Forster Fitzgerald Arbuthnot

Arabic Authors

A Manual of Arabian History and Literature

Forster Fitzgerald Arbuthnot

Arabic Authors
A Manual of Arabian History and Literature

ISBN/EAN: 9783744761680

Printed in Europe, USA, Canada, Australia, Japan

Cover: Foto ©ninafisch / pixelio.de

More available books at **www.hansebooks.com**

A Manual

OF

ARABIAN HISTORY AND LITERATURE.

BY

F. F. ARBUTHNOT, M.R.A.S.,

AUTHOR OF
"EARLY IDEAS" AND "PERSIAN PORTRAITS."

LONDON:
WILLIAM HEINEMANN.
1890.
[All rights reserved.]

PREFACE.

The following pages contain nothing new and nothing original, but they do contain a good deal of information gathered from various sources, and brought together under one cover. The book itself may be useful, not, perhaps, to the Professor or to the Orientalist, but to the general reader, and to the student commencing the study of Arabic. To the latter it will give some idea of the vast field of Arabian literature that lies before him, and prepare him, perhaps, for working out a really interesting work upon the subject. Such still remains to be written in the English language, and it is to be hoped that it will be done some day thoroughly and well.

It is gratifying to think that the study of Oriental languages and literature is progressing in Europe generally, if not in England particularly. The last Oriental Congress, held at Stockholm and Christiania the beginning of September, 1889, brought together a goodly number of Oriental scholars. There were twenty-eight nationalities represented altogether, and the many papers prepared and read, or taken as read preparatory to their being printed, showed that matters connected with Oriental studies in all their branches excite considerable interest.

England, too, has been lately making some efforts which will be, it is sincerely hoped, crowned with success. The lectures on modern Oriental languages lately established by the Imperial Institute of the United Kingdom, the Colonies, and India, in union with University College and King's College, London, is full of promise of bringing forth good fruit hereafter. So much is to be learnt from Oriental literature in various ways that it is to be hoped the day may yet come when the study of one or more Oriental languages will be taken up as a pastime to fill the leisure hours of a future generation thirsting after knowledge.

In addition to the above, a movement is also being made to attempt to revive the old Oriental Translation Fund. It was originally started in A.D. 1828, and did good work for fifty years, publishing translations (see Appendix) from fifteen different Oriental languages, and then collapsing from apathy, neglect, and want of funds. Unless well supported, both by donations and annual subscriptions, it is useless to attempt a fresh start. To succeed thoroughly it must be regarded as a national institution, and sufficiently well-off to be able to afford to bring out Texts and Indexes of vernacular books, and Translations of Oriental standard works, such as would not pay to be published by private individuals. It is doubtful whether sufficient money will ever be realized to undertake such an ambitious programme; but still something ought to be done in the matter, even though the proposal should not meet with success.

A final effort is, therefore, now being made. A committee has been appointed. Annual subscriptions and donations will be asked for, and, if these are promised in sufficient numbers and sufficient quantities, there is every chance of the undertaking being started on a sound and permanent basis. From India and England a sum of five thousand pounds ought to be forthcoming, the interest on which, along with a small annual subscription from several hundred subscribers, would be enough to redeem the character of Great Britain, and to strengthen the feeling that this country is not so entirely apathetic and neglectful in the encouragement of the study of Oriental literature as she is generally supposed to be.

With regard to Arabic literature in particular, a certain amount has been translated into English, but there remains a good deal of interesting matter still in the vernacular. The general catalogue of Arabic works published by Mr. Bernard Quaritch, 15, Piccadilly, and for sale at moderate prices, shows how much still remains untranslated. And of them certain historical and biographical works, and especially An-Nadim's 'Fihrist,' a most valuable book of reference, ought to be done into English without further delay. Private individuals can hardly undertake the business, but a well-organized and permanent Oriental Translation Fund, assisted by the English and Indian Governments, could and would render extraordinary services in the publication of texts, translations, and indexes of Oriental literature generally.

For assistance in the preparation of this present volume my thanks are due to the many authors whose works have been freely used and quoted, and also to Mr. E. Rehatsek, of Bombay, whose knowledge of the Arabic language and of Arabic literature is well known to all Oriental scholars.

F. F. ARBUTHNOT.

18, Park Lane, W.

CONTENTS.

CHAPTER I.

HISTORICAL.

Arabia: its boundaries, divisions of districts, revenues, area, population, and history.—Tribe of Koraish.—The Kaabah at Mecca.—Muhammad.—His immediate successors: Abu Bakr, Omar, Othman, Ali.—The Omaiyides.—Fate of Hasan and Hussain, sons of Ali.—Sunnis and Shiahs.—Overthrow of the Omaiyides by the Abbasides.—The Omaiyides in Spain; their conquests and government.—The Moors, and their final expulsion.—To what extent Europe is indebted to the Spanish Arabs.—Their literature and architecture.—The Abbaside Khalifs at Baghdad.—Persia, Egypt, Syria, Palestine, and Arabia become detached from their government in the course of time.—Fall of Baghdad itself in A.D. 1258.—Dealings of the Turks with Arabia.—The Wahhabi reform movement.—Expeditions of the Turks and Egyptians to suppress it.—Various defeats and successes.—Present form of government in Arabia.—Its future prospects.—List of the Omaiyide Khalifs, preceded by Muhammad and his four immediate successors.—List of the Abbaside Khalifs.—List of the Arab rulers in Spain 1

CHAPTER II.

LITERARY.

About the Arabic and Chinese languages.—The permanent character of the former attributed to the Koran.—Division of Arab literature into three periods: I. The time before Muhammad.—The sage Lokman; the description of three Lokmans; Arab poetry before the Koran; the seven suspended poems, known as the Mua'llakat, at Mecca; notions of the Arabs about poetry; their Kasidas; description of the Kasidas of Amriolkais, Antara, Labid, Tarafa, Amru, Harath, and Zoheir; the poets Nabiga, Al-Kama, and Al-Aasha. II. The period from the time of Muhammad to the fall of the Abbasides.—Muhammad considered as a poet; the poets who were hostile to him; his panegyrist Kab bin Zoheir; account of him and his 'Poem of the Mantle,' and the results; Al-Busiri's 'Poem of the Mantle;' names of poets favourable and hostile to Muhammad; the seven jurisconsults; the four imams; the six fathers of tradition; the early traditionists; the companions; the alchemists; the astronomers; the grammarians; the geographers and travellers; the historians; the tabulators and biographers; the writers about natural history; the philologists; the philosophers; the physicians; the poets; the collectors and editors of poems; the essayist Al-Hariri; many translators; special notice of Ibn Al-Mukaffa; support given to learning and literature by certain of the Omaiyide, Abbaside, and Spanish Arab Khalifs; description of Baghdad; reign of Harun-ar-Raschid; the Barmekides; the Khalif Razi-billah; Hakim II. at Cordova; his education; his accession to the throne; his collection of books; his library, and its catalogue; places of learning in the East at this time. III. Third period, from the fall of Baghdad to the present time.—Certain historians; Ibn Malik, the grammarian; Ibn Batuta, the traveller; Abul Feda, Ibn Khaldun, Ibn Kesir, Ibn Hajar, Ibn Arabshah—all historians; Firuzabadi, Taki-uddin of Fez, Al-Makrisi, Sayuti, Ibn Kamal Pasha, Abu Sa'ud the mufti, Ibrahim of Aleppo, Birgeli, Abul Khair; celebrated caligraphers, past and present, Haji Khalfa, Muhammad al Amin of Damascus, Makkari. Decline of Arabic literature: its present form. About the printing-presses of Arabic works at various places . . . 23

CHAPTER III.

ABOUT MUHAMMAD.

A complete summary of the details of his life, from his birth to his death.—Remarks upon him as a reformer, preacher, and apostle.—The Hanyfs.—Muhammad's early idea of establishing one religion for the Jews, Christians, and Arabs.—His long struggle with the Koraish.—His failure at Mecca.—His success at Madinah.—Adapts his views to the manners and customs of the Arabs only.—The reason of his many marriages.—His love of women.—About the Koran. —Not collected and arranged until after his death.— Comparison of the Koran with the Old and New Testaments.—Superiority of our Bible.—Description of it by ' Il Secolo.'—Rev. Mr. Badger's description of the Koran.—Written in the purest Arabic, and defies competition.—Muhammad and Moses, Jesus and Buddha.—Remarks about Buddhism and Christianity.—Moses and Muhammad the founders of two nationalities. — Abraham the father of the Jewish, Christian, and Muhammadan religions.— Rénan's description of the gods of the Jews.— Joseph.—The Twelve Tribes. —Appearance of Moses as a liberator and organizer.—The reasons of his wanderings in the desert.—What the Jews owed to Moses, and the Arabs to Muhammad.—The latter as a military leader.—Resemblance of the warlike expeditions of the Jews and of the Arabs.—Similar proceedings in the Soudan at the present time.—Account of the dogmas and precepts of Islam as embodied in the Koran.—Other points connected with the institutions of Islam.—Faith and prayer always insisted upon.—Democratic character of the Muhammadan religion, excellent in theory, but doubtful in practice.—Muhammad's last address at Mina, telling the Muslims that they were one brotherhood.—His final remarks . . 119

CHAPTER IV.

TALES AND STORIES.

The Kalilah wa Dimnah.—'Early Ideas.'—'Persian Portraits.'—Origin of the 'Arabian Nights.'—The Hazar Afsaneh, or Thousand Stories. Date of the 'Nights.'—Its fables and apologues the oldest part of the work.—Then certain stories—The latest tales.—Galland's edition.—His biography.—His successors, sixeen in number, ending with Payne and Burton.—The complete translations of these two last-named, in thirteen and sixteen volumes respectively.—Brief analysis of Payne's first nine, and of Burton's first ten volumes.—Short summary of twelve stories; viz.: The tale of Aziz and Azizah; the tale of Kamar Al-Zaman and the Lady Budur; Ala Aldin Abu Al-Shamat; Ali the Persian and the Kurd sharper; the man of Al-Yaman and his six slave-girls; Abu Al-Husn and his slave-girl Tawaddud; the rogueries of Dalilah the Crafty and her daughter Zeynab the Trickstress; the adventures of Quicksilver Ali of Cairo; Hasan of Busra and the king's daughter of the Jinn; Ali Nur Al-din and Miriam the girdle-girl; Kamar Al Zaman and the jeweller's wife; Ma'aruf the cobbler and his wife Fatimah. Remarks on Payne's three extra volumes, entitled 'Tales from the Arabic,' and on Burton's two first supplemental volumes.—Allusion to Burton's third supplemental and to Payne's thirteenth volume.—Burton's fourth, fifth, and sixth supplemental volumes.—Summing-up of the number of stories contained in the above two editions; from what manuscripts they were translated, and some final remarks.—The Kathá Sarit Ságara, a sort of Hindoo 'Arabian Nights'.—Comparison of the two works.—Brief description of the Kathá and its contents.—Gunádhya and Somadeva.—Final remarks on the stories found in the Kathá.—Antar, a Bedouin romance.—Its partial translation.—Its supposed author.—Brief description of the work, with some remarks upon it.—Both the 'Arabian Nights' and Antar rather long.—The press in England to-day.—Numerous writers of novels and story-books.—These take the place of the 'Nights,' and satisfy the public, always in search of something new, even if not true; something original, even if not trustworthy.—Final remarks 151

CHAPTER V.

ANECDOTES AND ANA.

In Persian literature the Gulistan, Negaristan, and Beharistan contain many anecdotes.—In Arabic literature there are works of the same kind.—'The Naphut-ul-Yaman,' or Breath of Yaman.—Six stories translated from it.—The Merzuban namah, with newly translated extracts from it.—Remarks on this work.—The Al-Mustatraf, or the Gleaner or the Collector.—Two stories from it.—Two anecdotes taken from the Sehr-ul-oyoon, or Magic of the Eyes.—A philosophic discourse, translated from the Siraj-ul-Muluk, or Lamp of Kings.—The Ilam en Nas, or Warnings for Men.—Eighteen stories from Ibn Khallikan's Biographical Dictionary.—Seven anecdotes from various sources.—Verses from the

Arabic about the places where certain Arabs wished to be buried.—Translation of the verses upon Alfred de Musset's tomb in Paris	188
APPENDIX . .	235
INDEX	239

ARABIC AUTHORS.

CHAPTER I.

HISTORICAL.

THE Arabia of to-day is bounded on the west by the Red Sea and Gulf of Suez; on the south by the Gulf of Aden and the Arabian Sea; on the east by the Gulf of Oman and the Persian Gulf; and on the north by a portion of Syria. This last boundary would, however, be more clearly defined by drawing a line from Suez straight across to the western head of the Persian Gulf.

By the Greeks and Romans this country was divided into Arabia Petræa, Arabia Deserta, and Arabia Felix, or the Stony, the Desert, and the Happy. The Arabs themselves call it 'The Land of the Arabs,' while modern geographers give the Sinaitic peninsula as the first geographic district; the Hijaz, including the Haram, or sacred territory of Mecca, as the second; and Yaman, with the Tehamah, as the third. To these may be added the provinces of Hadramaut and Mahrah, and of Oman and Hasa, to the south and east respectively, with Nejd, or Central Arabia, as the central plateau, and some large deserts scattered in different parts of the peninsula.

Of the revenues of Arabia it is almost impossible to form anything like a correct estimate. The area of the country covers about 1,200,000 square miles, and the population is said to be from five to six millions, of whom one-fifth consist of Ahl Bedoo, or dwellers in the open land, otherwise known as Bedouins; and four-fifths of settled Arabs, called Ahl Hadr, or dwellers in fixed localities.

The history of Arabia may be divided into three periods:

1st. The prehistoric period, full of tales of heroes, and giants, and wonderful cities.

2nd. The period which preceded the era of Muhammad.

3rd. That which followed it.

The first period is mythical to a certain extent; at all events, nothing can be stated positively about it. The second period is distinguished as one of local monarchies and federal governments in a rough and rude form; while the third commences with theocratic centralization, dissolving finally into general anarchy.

Of the many tribes in Arabia, the most celebrated is the family of the Koraish, still regarded as the noblest of the Arabs, partly because, at the beginning of the fifth century A.D., their chiefs had rendered themselves the masters and acknowledged guardians of the sacred Kaabah at Mecca, and partly because of their connection with the Prophet. The Kaabah, La Maison Carrée, or square temple, a shrine of unknown antiquity, was situated within the precincts of the town of Mecca, and to it, long before Muhammad's time, the Arabs had brought yearly offerings, and made devout pilgrimages. The tribe of Koraish, having once obtained the keys of the consecrated building, had held them against all comers till Muhammad's conquest of Mecca in A.D. 630, when he handed over the key to Othman bin Talha, the former custodian, to be kept by him and his posterity as an hereditary and perpetual office, and he further confirmed his uncle Abbas in the office of giving drink to the pilgrims.

Before entering into a somewhat lengthy description of Arabian literature, it is necessary to give a short and rapid sketch of Arabian history, beginning from the time of Muhammad, as his Koran was the foundation of the literary edifice. All Arab authors have looked upon that work as the height of eloquent diction, and have regarded it as the model standard to be followed in all their productions. Leaving, then, the two first periods of Arabian history, viz., the prehistoric, and the pre-Muhammadan, without any particular notice, the third period will be sketched as briefly as possible, and will be found excessively interesting, containing as it does the rise, grandeur, and decline of the Arabs as a nation.

Muhammad, on his death in June, A.D. 632, left the entire Arab peninsula, with two or three exceptions, under one sceptre and one creed. He was succeeded by Abu Bakr (the father of Ayesha, the favourite wife of the prophet), known as the Companion of the Cave, with the title of Khalifah, or successor. His reign only lasted two years, but during that period the various insurrections that broke out in Arabia in consequence of the death of the Prophet were promptly put down, after severe fighting, in various parts of the peninsula, and the whole country was subjugated. Foreign expeditions beyond the borders were also planned and started.

Abu Bakr, dying in August, A.D. 634, was succeeded by Umar, or Omar, the conqueror of Syria, Persia, and Egypt by means of his generals Khalid bin Walid (the best, perhaps, that Islam produced), Abu Obaida, Mothanna, Sád bin Malik, Amr bin al-Aási, and others. Omar himself was an early convert of A.D. 615, and a sudden conversion like our Paul; but one made his converts by fanaticism and the sword, the other by preaching and the pen. After a glorious and victorious reign of ten years Omar was assassinated by a Persian slave in November, A.D. 644, and was followed as Khalif by Othman, son of Affan, of the noble family of Abd-esh-Shems, who also assumed the title 'Amir al-Momenin,' or Commander of the Faithful, which had been first adopted by his predecessor Omar. Othman ruled for twelve years, when he was murdered in A.D. 656, some say at the instigation of Ali, nephew of Muhammad, and husband of his only daughter Fatima. Anyhow, Ali succeeded Othman as Khalif, but was defeated by Moawia, Governor of Syria, and assassinated in A.D. 660.

Moawia bin Abu Sofyan then established the Benou Umayya dynasty, called by Europeans the Omaiyides, or Ommiades, from the name of Umayya, the father of the race. This dynasty reigned for nearly ninety years, and numbered fourteen successive princes, with their capital at Damascus.

During the reign of Yazid I., the second prince (A.D. 679-683), Hussain, the younger son of Ali the Khalif, came to an untimely end. His elder brother, Hasan, a man of quiet disposition, had been previously murdered by one of his wives, at the instigation, it is said, of Yazid before he came to the throne. This happened in A.D. 669. Later on Hussain, with his followers, rose in rebellion, and was killed on the plain of Kerbela, A.D. 680. The descendants, however, of this faction continued the disturbances which eventually brought about the great Muhammadan schism, and the splitting up of the religion into two sects, known to this day as the Sunnis and Shias. The adherents of the legitimate Khalifate, and of the orthodox doctrine, assumed the name of Sunnites, or Traditionists. These acknowledge the first four Khalifs (the rightly minded, or rightly directed, as they are called) to have been legitimate successors of Muhammad, while the sectaries of Ali are known as the Shiites, or Separatists. These last regard Ali as the first rightful Imam, for they prefer this title (found in Sura ii., verse 118, of the Koran) to that of Khalif. The Turks and Arabs are Sunnis; the Persians, and most of the Muhammadans of India, Shias.

This division into two sects, who hate each other cordially, has done more to weaken the power of the Muhammadan religion as a power than anything else. The Shias to this day execrate the memory of Yazid as the murderer of their hero Hussain, whom they have ever regarded as a martyr, and given full vent to their feelings on the subject in their ' Passion Play,' translated by Sir Lewis Pelly, and described by Mr. Benjamin in his ' Persia and the Persians.'

Other insurrections against the reigning Omaiyide Khalifs were also put down, portions of Asia, Africa and Spain conquered, and even France invaded, so that at the close of the Benou Umayya dynastry, about A.D. 750, their empire consisted of many and large territories in Europe, Africa and Asia. Their colour was white, as opposed to the black of the Abbasides, and the green of the Fatimites, as descendants of Muhammad.

But the Benou Umayya dynasty succumbed,

A.D. 749, under the blows of Ibrahim (great-grandson of Abbas, the uncle of the Prophet), and of his younger brother, Abul Abbas, better known in history as As-Saffah, or the Blood-shedder. A decisive battle was fought on the banks of the river Zab, near Arbela, and Marwan II. (A.D. 744-750), the last of the Omaiyide Khalifs, was defeated, and fled first to Damascus, and then to Egypt, where he was eventually killed by his pursuers, A.D. 750.

The history of the reign of the Abbasides now begins, and under them the power and glory of Islam reached their highest point. But it is first necessary to allude to the conquest of Spain by the Omaiyides, a branch of which family still retained for a long time in the West the power which they had totally lost in the East.

The most important achievement of the reign of Walid I. (A.D. 705-715), the sixth prince of the Omaiyide dynasty, was the conquest of Spain by his generals Tarik and Musa. The Arabs (known in Europe under the name of Saracens) first established themselves in Cordova about A.D. 711, and the two generals above named continued their victorious progress throughout the country in 712 and 713, until nearly nine-tenths of the peninsula was held by the Muhammadans.

Some years later France even was invaded by the Arabs, and the banners of the Muslims were erected on the coasts of the Gulf of Lyons, on the

walls of Narbonne, of Nimes, of Carcassonne, and of
Béziers. The Arabs afterwards advanced as far as
the plains of Tours, where their victorious progress
was checked by Charles Martel, who gained a
great victory over them near that town in October,
A.D. 732, and completely defeated them, so that
they were obliged to retire again to Spain. There
successive viceroys and emirs ruled as the repre-
sentatives of the Khalifs at Damascus until the
fall of the Omaiyide dynasty in the East, A.D. 750.

But even after that Spain remained for many
years under Arab domination. Anarchy almost
prevailed from A.D. 750 to 755, but in that year
the Arabs of Spain, weary of disorder, elected as
their ruler Abd-ar-Rahman, grandson of the
Khalif Hashim, tenth prince of the Omaiyide
dynasty. At the time of his election, Abd-ar-
Rahman was a wanderer in the desert, pursued by
his enemies, when a deputation from Andalusia
sought him out and offered him the Khalifate of
Spain. It was gladly accepted. He landed there
in September, A.D. 755, was universally welcomed,
and founded at Cordova the Western Omaiyide
Khalifate, which lasted up to A.D. 1031, under
sixteen rulers, with certain interruptions during
the reign of the last seven of them. On the
extinction of the Khalifate, Spain was broken up
into various petty kingdoms under kings and
kinglets belonging to different Arab tribes and
families. This continued from A.D. 1032 to 1092,

when the Almoravides established themselves from
A.D. 1092 to 1147, and were followed by the
Almohades, who reigned up to A.D. 1232.

After this Cordova, Seville, and other places
were taken by Ferdinand III. of Leon and Castile,
between A.D. 1236 and 1248. On the fall of
Cordova the Muhammadan power declined with
great rapidity ; and, though the celebrated kingdom
of Granada was established by the Moors in A.D.
1232, it was their last refuge from the rising
power of the Christians. Some twenty-one princes
reigned there till A.D. 1492, when Granada itself
was taken, and this last Muhammadan dynasty was
driven out of Spain by Ferdinand of Arragon and
Isabella of Castile. Thus ended the empire of
the Arabs and the Moors in Spain, which had
lasted nearly eight hundred years.

The Spanish Arabs were extremely fond of learning. Indeed, it is due to them to a very great
extent that literature and science were kept afloat
in Europe during the ages that followed the invasion
of the Barbarians, as the Huns, Vandals, Goths,
and Visigoths were generally called. That interval known as the 'Dark Ages' was kept alight
by the Arabs alone. Abd-ar-Rahman II. established a library at Cordova during his reign, A.D.
822-852. Hakim II., the successor of Abd-ar-
Rahman III., loved the sciences, founded the
University of Cordova, and collected a library of
great magnitude (A.D. 961-976).

The revival of learning in Europe is chiefly attributed to the writings of Arabian doctors and philosophers, and to the schools which they founded in several parts of Spain and Italy. These seats of learning were frequented even in the twelfth century of our era by students from various parts of Europe, who disseminated the knowledge thus acquired when they returned to their own countries. At that time many Arabic works were translated into Latin, which thus facilitated the progress of science. In the three last chapters of the second book of the 'History of the Muhammadan Dynasties in Spain,' translated by Pascual de Gayangos, the state of science and literature is detailed in the words of Makkari, the original Arab author of that work, and in it many once celebrated authors are mentioned, of whom not only their productions, but even their very names, have since perished. The distinguished writers whose works have come down to us will be more particularly alluded to in the next chapter. Europe is also indebted to the Arabs for the elements of many useful sciences, particularly that of chemistry. Paper was first made in Europe by them, and their carpets and manufactures in steel and leather were long unrivalled, while in the Arabian schools of Cordova mathematics, astronomy, philosophy, botany and medicine were taught with great success.

As Europe gradually emerged from darkness and ignorance, the Moors in Spain became so weak and powerless that in A.D. 1526 Charles I. of Spain, and V. of Germany, ordered them to adopt the Spanish language. In A.D. 1566 an edict of Philip II. forbade them to speak or write in Arabic, and directed them to renounce all their traditional habits, customs and ceremonies. Philip III. completed the work which his father had left unfinished. In A.D. 1609 all the Moriscoes were ordered to depart from the peninsula within three days, with a penalty of death if they failed to obey the order, and from that time their existence as a nation finally ceased in Europe, and Spain thus lost a million of industrious inhabitants skilled in the useful arts. After their expulsion Arabic literature more or less disappeared. Much of it was destroyed, and a Spanish cardinal, it is said, once boasted that he had destroyed with his own hands one hundred thousand Arabic manuscripts! It is highly probable that the remnants of Andalusian libraries were brought to light by Casiri (b. 1710, d. 1791) during the past, and by Gayangos during the present century, and it is doubtful if much more will ever now be discovered.

There are two buildings still extant in Spain which have survived the Arabs, viz., their mosque at Cordova (now the Cathedral), and their palace of the Alhambra at Granada, both well worth a visit, and well described in Murray's and O'Shea's guides to Spain. During the reign of Abd-ar-Rahman III. (A.D. 912-961) the city, palace, and gardens of Medinatu-z-Ahra, three or four miles from Cordova, were constructed in honour of his favourite wife or mistress, Az-zahra, and cost an immense sum of money. At present no vestiges of them exist, and it is supposed that not only these, but many other Arab mosques and buildings, were intentionally destroyed by their conquerors, as the hatred between the Christian and the Muslim in those days was of the bitterest description.

And now to return to the Abbasides, established in the East on the downfall of the Omaiyide dynasty there in A.D. 750, and thus continue the main line of Arab history.

There were, in all, thirty-seven Abbaside Khalifs, of whom Abu Jaafar, surnamed Al-Mansur, the Victorious (A.D. 754-775), Harun-ar-Rashid (A.D. 786-809), and Al-Mamun (A.D. 812-833) were the most celebrated. Of these, the first, who was the second Khalif, founded Baghdad, the capital of the Abbasides, about A.D. 762 ; the second, who was the fifth Khalif, has been rendered immortal by the frequent illusions to him, and to members of the Barmeki family, in the 'Arabian Nights'; while the third, who was the seventh Khalif, was a great patron of literature and science.

As years rolled on the dynasty and its princes became weaker and weaker, and finally came to an end under the thirty-seventh and last Khalif Al-Mustaa'sim Billah, with the capture of Baghdad in A.D. 1258 by Halaku Khan, the sovereign of the Mughals, and the grandson of Jenghiz Khan.

Long before this, however, the empire which the first of the Abbasides had conquered was already broken up. About A.D. 879, in Persia, Amr-bin-Lais founded the Suffary or Braiser dynasty, still subject to the Commander of the Faithful. But even this allegiance only lasted till A.D. 901, when the Samani and Dailami dynasties were established in the North and South of Persia respectively, and quite independent of the Khalifs of Baghdad.

In A.D. 909, the Fatimites, so designated from one Obaid Allah, a real or pretended descendant of Ali and Fatima, the daughter of Muhammad, established themselves in the North of Africa, and consolidated their power there. In A.D. 972 Al-Moizz, or Abu Tamim, a great-grandson of Obaid Allah, the founder of the Fatimite dynasty at Tunis, sent his general Jawhar with an army to invade Egypt. The country was conquered, the city of Cairo built, the seat of government was transferred there, and the title of Khalif assumed by the Fatimites. There they remained as reigning Khalifs until A.D 1171, when Salah-ad-Din (Saladin) usurped the sovereignty, and founded the Ayoobite dynasty of Kurds, till its last ruler, Melik-al-Ashraf, was deposed in A.D. 1250 by the Mamlook El Moizz, who in that year founded the Baharite Mamlook dynasty, which lasted with variations in the families till A.D. 1377. But in

A.D. 1260 Ez-Zahir Beybars, a Mamlook slave, secured the throne, and brought the then representative of the Abbaside Khalifs (the family having been dethroned by the Mughals at Baghdad in A.D. 1258) to Egypt, and recognised him as possessing spiritual authority alone, but nothing else. From that time until the taking of Egypt by Sultan Selim I. in A.D. 1517, the Abbaside Khalifs retained the spiritual power first under the Baharite, and then under the Circassian or Borgite Mamlooks. When Egypt became a Turkish pashalic, Selim, the conqueror, compelled the representative of the Abbaside Khalifs, by name Al-Motawukkel, to leave Cairo and reside in Constantinople; and on his death the Ottoman Sultans assumed the title of Khalif, which they hold to this day, and are recognised by the Sunnis as the head of the Muhammadan religion, and the successors of Muhammad.

As regards Syria and Palestine (two countries more or less closely connected, owing to their proximity and absence of distinct and defined boundaries), on the termination of the rule of the Omaiyides at Damascus in A.D. 750, they remained nominally under the Abbasides till A.D. 969, when Syria was conquered by the Fatimites, who were succeeded by the Seljuks, who captured Damascus about A.D. 1075, and Antioch A.D. 1085. The struggles with the Crusaders commenced in A.D. 1096, and continued until Saladin's famous victory at Hattin in 1187, when he became master of nearly the whole of Syria and Palestine. Fighting still went on in these countries between the Franks and others until A.D. 1518, when Selim I. conquered the country and incorporated it with the Turkish Empire. No Arab prince has since reigned in Egypt or Syria, though these countries have always exercised certain influences over Arabia.

In Arabia itself, towards the end of the tenth century and the beginning of the eleventh, A.D., the Karmathians had risen in revolt, and detached that country from the Abbaside dynasty to such an extent that she returned almost to her primitive independence. Indeed, it may be said that, in the whole of Arabia, the Hijaz, with the Haram, or sacred territory of Mecca, under the Shariff, or nobles, the lineal descendants of the tribe of Koraish, alone retained some kind of constituted authority, and paid allegiance sometimes to the government of Baghdad, and sometimes to that of Egypt.

As already stated above, in A.D. 1517 the Turkish Sultan Selim I. conquered Egypt, and obtained from the last real, or supposed surviving, Abbaside kinsman of the Prophet a formal investiture of the Muhammadan Khalifate. This was more religious than political in its bearing, but still many of the tribes in Arabia offered their allegiance to the Ottoman Government.

From that time the Turks began their dealings with Arabia, which remained in a sort of independence under their own tribal Shaikhs, more or less according to the circumstances of different districts, until the rise of the Wahhabi movement, about the middle of the eighteenth century of our era.

The Wahhabi reform movement requires special mention. It began in Arabia about A.D. 1740. The reformer and originator of the movement was Muhammad bin Abdul Wahhab, born at the town of Aïnah, in the centre of the Nejd district, A.D. 1691. He died in A.D. 1787, aged ninety-six. After some years spent in travel and in study, he began his preaching about A.D. 1731. Driven from Aïnah, his native place, as Muhammad was driven from Mecca, Abdul Wahhab established himself at ad-Diriyyah, where Muhammad bin Saood, the Shaikh of a sub-tribe of the Anizeh, gave him shelter, and eventually married his daughter. By preaching and fighting, his followers increased in number, and his reforms spread throughout the Nejd district, and many converts were made by him and his successors.

In A.D. 1797 a Turkish army from Baghdad attacked the Wahhabis, but were beaten, and two years later Saood II. took and plundered Kerbela, Taïf, Mecca, and other places, and seems to have retained his power and his government for several years.

In A.D. 1811 the Turks, who had quite lost their authority in Arabia, requested Muhammad Ali of Egypt to put down the movement, and reconquer the country. The first expedition, commanded by his son Tussun, in its attempt to take Madinah, was nearly annihilated, but succeeded the following year. Later on the campaign was conducted by Muhammad Ali in person, and afterwards by his adopted son Ibrahim Pasha, with considerable success. The final stronghold, ad-Diriyyah, was captured in A.D. 1818, the Wahhabi chief captured, and sent first to Egypt and then to Constantinople, where he was beheaded in December of that year.

The Egyptian occupation of Arabia was followed by a renewal of the Wahhabi movement, which eventually succeeded, in A.D. 1842, in driving out the Egyptians, occupied as they were at the time with fighting the Turks in Syria and Anatolia. Wahhabism was then re-established in some parts, and independence in other parts, of the country; but on the whole Wahhabism has never been very popular either in Arabia or India, in which latter country it also has some followers. It may be regarded as the latest sect of Islam, but does not make much progress.

Arabia may now be said to be under three different kinds of government—*i.e.*, partly under the Wahhabis, partly under the Turks, and partly under independent rulers, while Aden has been held by the English ever since its first capture in A.D. 1839. In other words, the present position of Arabia may be more definitely described as follows: Hasa, Hareek, the whole of Nejd, Kaseem, the provinces adjoining Yaman on the north, and Aseer, forming a broad belt, and stretching across the centre of the peninsula from the Red Sea to the Persian Gulf, remain under Wahhabi influences. The Hijaz and some sea-ports, such as Jedda and others, are at present absolutely under the Turkish Government; while Bahrein, Oman and its capital Muscat, and Yaman are more or less independent. Between Nejd and Syria a new and promising kingdom has sprung up under Telal.

The time perhaps may come, and perhaps not far distant, when the Turks will disappear altogether from Arabia, and Wahhabism and independent tribes will alone remain. Another Muhammad or another Abdul Wahhab may some day again appear, and bring together the tribes under one rule for a time. It is doubtful, though, if ever the Arabs will again have the power, talent, or enthusiasm to revive the glories of the Arabian Empire, which now lives in history only, and is well worth a study.

For ready reference the following is a chronology of the dynasty of the Omaiyides, preceded by Muhammad and the first Khalifahs:

	A.D.	
Muhammad the Apostle	622	632
Abu Bakr	632	634

	A.D.
Omar I.	634—643
Othman	643—655
Ali	655—660
1. Moawia I.	660—679
2. Yazid I.	679—683
3. Moawia II.	683—683
4. Marwan I.	683—684
5. Abdul-Malik	684—705
6. Walid I.	705—715
7. Sulaiman	715—717
8. Omar II.	717—720
9. Yazid II.	720—724
10. Hashim	724—743
11. Walid II.	743—744
12. Yazid III.	744—744
13. Ibrahim	744—744
14. Marwan II.	744—750

The dynasty of the Omaiyides was followed by that of the Abbasides, who reigned as follows:

	A.D.
1. Abul-Abbas As-Saffah	750—754
2. Al-Mansur	754—775
3. Al-Mahdi	775—785
4. Al-Hadi	785—786
5. Harun-ar-Rashid	786—809
6. Al-Amin	809—812
7. Al-Mâmun	812—833
8. Al-Mo'tasim Billah	833—842
9. Al-Wathik	842—847
10. Al-Mutwakkil	847—861
11. Al-Mustansir Billah	861—862
12. Al-Mustain Billah	862—866
13. Al-Mo'tiz Billah	866—869
14. Al-Muhtadi Billah	869—870
15. Al-Mo'tamid	870—892
16. Al-Motazid Billah	892—902
17. Al-Muktafi Billah	902—908
18. Al-Muktadir Billah	908—932

					A.D.
19.	Al-Kahir Billah	-	-	-	932—934
20.	Al-Radhï Billah	-	-	-	934—940
21.	Al-Muttaki Billah	-	-	-	940—944
22.	Al-Mustakfi Billah	-	-	-	944—945
23.	Al-Mutia Billah	-	-	-	945—974
24.	Al-Taya Billah	-	-	-	974—991
25.	Al-Kadir Billah	-	-	-	991—1031
26.	Al-Kaim Billah	-	-	-	1031—1075
27.	Al-Muktadi Billah	-	-	-	1075—1094
28.	Al-Mustazhir Billah	-	-	-	1094—1118
29.	Al-Mustershid Billah	-	-	-	1118—1135
30.	Al-Rashid Billah	-	-	-	1135—1136
31.	Al-Muktafi	-	-	-	1136—1160
32.	Al-Mustanjid Billah	-	-	-	1160—1170
33.	Al-Mustazi	-	-	-	1170—1180
34.	Al-Nasir Billah	-	-	-	1180—1225
35.	Al-Tahir	-	-	-	1225—1226
36.	Al-Mustansir Billah II.	-	-	-	1226—1240
37.	Al-Mustaa'sim Billah	-	-	-	1240—1258

killed at the taking of Baghdad by Halaku Khan, and the last of the dynasty, which continued, however, as a spiritual power in Egypt till A.D. 1517.

The empire over which the Abbasides began to rule in A.D. 750 had gradually dwindled away until little but Baghdad and its environs were left on the fall of the dynasty in A.D. 1258. Will history repeat itself in the same way as regards Constantinople, which in some years may be the only territory left in Europe to a people who once were conquerors, and whose arms even were carried to the walls of Vienna? As Persia, Egypt, Syria, parts of Africa and Arabia, by degrees, were severed from the Abbaside Empire, so the different provinces of Turkey in Europe appear to be slowly separating themselves from the Turkish Power, until finally there will be nothing left to them in Europe but that city whose splendid position will ever make it a bone of contention to both rising and declining States.

The following is a list of the Omaiyides who ruled in Spain A.D. 756 to 1031 :

		A.D.
1. Abd-ar-Rahman I.	- - -	756—788
2. Hisham I.	- - -	788—796
3. Al-Hakim I.	- - -	796—822
4. Abd-ar-Rahman II.	- - -	822—852
5. Muhammad I.	- -	852—886
6. Al-Mundhir	- - -	886—888
7. Abd-Allah	- - -	888—912
8. Abd-ar-Rahman III.	- - -	912—961

one of the greatest of the rulers of Cordova. Under this prince, who at last assumed the title of Khalif and Commander of the Faithful, the unity of Muhammadan Spain was for the time restored.

		A.D.
9. Al-Hakim II.	- - -	961—976
10. Hisham II.	- - -	976—1009

a Khalif only in name, while Muhammad Bin Ali Amir, surnamed Al-Mansur, was the real ruler or regent till his death in A.D. 1002. He was succeeded by his son, Abd-al-Malik, who ruled successfully till his death in A.D. 1008, and was followed by his brother, Abd-ar-Rahman, who was beheaded in A.D. 1009, Hisham II. having been previously deposed.

	A.D.
11. Muhammad II. (Al-Mahdi-billah)	1009—1009
12. Sulaiman	1009—1010
Hisham II. for the second time	1010—1013
Sulaiman for the second time	1013—1016
(1) Ali bin Hammud, a Berber chief	1016—1018
13. Abd-ar-Rahman IV.	1018—1019
(2) Al Kasim bin Hammud	1019—1023
14. Abd-ar-Rahman V.	1023—1024
15. Muhammad III.	1024—1025
(3) Yabya bin Ali bin Hammud	1025—1027
16. Hisham III.	1027—1031

A complete list of all the Muhammadan rulers in Spain will be found in Makkari's history of these dynasties, translated by Gayangos.

CHAPTER II.

LITERARY.

THE oral communications of the ancient Egyptians, Medes and Persians, the two classic tongues of Europe, the Sanscrit of the Hindus and the Hebrew of the Jews, have long since ceased to be living languages. For the last twelve centuries no Western language has preserved its grammar, its style, or its literature intact and intelligible to the people of the present day. But two Eastern tongues have come down from ages past to our own times, and continue to exist unchanged in books, and, to a certain extent, also unchanged in language, and these are Chinese and Arabic. In China, though the dialects differ in the various provinces of the empire, still the written language has remained the same for centuries. In Arabia the Arabic language has retained its originality without very much dialectical alteration.

The unchangeable character of the Arabic language is chiefly to be attributed to the Koran, which has, from its promulgation to the present time, been regarded by all Muhammadans as the standard of religion and of literary composition. Strictly speaking, not only the history, but also the literature of the Arabs begins with Muhammad. Excepting the Mua'llakat, and other pre-Islamitic poems collected in the Hamasas of Abu Tammam and Al-Bohtori, in Ibn. Kutaiba and in the Mofaddhaliat, no literary monuments that preceded his time are in existence. The Koran became, not only the code of religious and of civil law, but also the model of the Arabic language, and the standard of diction and eloquence. Muhammad himself scorned metrical rules; he claimed as an apostle and lawgiver a title higher than that of soothsayer and poet. Still, his poetic talent is manifest in numerous passages of the Koran, well known to those able to read it in the original, and in this respect the last twenty-five chapters of that book are, perhaps, the most remarkable.

Although the power of the Arabs has long ago succumbed, their literature has survived, and their language is still more or less spoken in all Muhammadan countries. Europe at one time was lightened by the torch of Arabian learning, and the Middle Ages were stamped with the genius and character of Arab civilization. The great masters of philosophy, medicine, astronomy, and mathematics, viz., Al-Kindi, Al-Farabi, Ibn-Sina, Ibn-Rashid, Ibn Bajah, Razi, Al Battani, Abul Ma'shar, Al-Farghani, Al-Jaber, have been studied both in the

Spanish universities and in those of the rest of Europe, where their names are still familiar under the corrupted forms of Alchendius, Alfarabius, Avicenna, Averroes, Avempace, Rhazes, Albategnius, Albumasar, Alfraganius, and Geber.

Arabic literature commenced about half a century before Muhammad with a legion of poets. The seven poems suspended in the temple of Mecca, and of which more anon, were considered as the chief productions of that time. The Mussulman era begins with the Hijrah, or emigration of Muhammad from Mecca to Madinah, which is supposed to have taken place on the 20th of June, A.D. 622; and the rise, growth, and decay of Arab power, learning, and literature may be divided into three periods as follows :

1. The time before Muhammad.

2. From Muhammad and his immediate successors, viz., Abu Bakr, Omar, Othman, and Ali, through the Omaiyide and Abbaside dynasties, to the end of the Khalifate of Baghdad, A.D. 1258.

3. From the fall of Baghdad to the present time.

FIRST PERIOD.

Although the proper history of Arabian literature begins from the time of Muhammad, it is necessary to cast a glance upon the age that preceded him, in order to obtain a glimpse of pre-Islamitic wisdom. The sage Lokman, whose name the thirty-first chapter of the Koran bears, is considered, according to that book, to have been the first man of his nation who practised and taught wisdom in all his deeds and words. He was believed to have been a contemporary of David and Solomon; his sayings and his fables still exist, but there is not much really known about him, as the following extracts will show:

'Lokman, a philosopher mentioned in the Koran, is said to have been born about the time of David. One tradition represents him as a descendant of the Arab tribe of Ad, who, on account of his piety and wisdom, was saved when the rest of his family perished by Divine wrath. According to another story he was an Ethiopian slave, noted alike for bodily deformity and a gift for composing fables and apologues. This account of Lokman, resembling so closely the traditional history of Æsop, has led to an opinion that they were the same individual, but this is now generally supposed not to be the case. The various reports agree in ascribing to Lokman extraordinary longevity. His extant fables bear evident marks of modern alteration, both in their diction and their incidents. They were first published with a Latin translation of the Arabic by Erpenius (Leyden, 1615). Galland produced a French translation of the fables of Lokman and Bidpay at Paris in 1724, and there are other editions by De Sacey, 1816, Caussin de

Perceval, 1818, Freytag, 1823, and Rodiger, 1830.'

Burton, in a footnote to page 118, of Volume X. of his 'Arabian Nights,' however, says that 'There are three distinct Lokmans. The first, or eldest Lokman, entitled Al-Hakim (the Sage), and the hero of the Koranic chapter which bears his name, was son of Ba'ura, of the children of Azar, sister's son to Job, or son of Job's maternal aunt; he witnessed David's miracles of mail-making, and when the tribe of Ad was destroyed he became king of the country. The second Lokman, also called the Sage, was a slave and Abyssinian negro, sold by the Israelites during the reign of David or Solomon, and who left a volume of proverbs and exempla, not fables or apologues, some of which still dwell in the public memory. The youngest Lokman, of the Vultures, was a prince of the tribe of Ad, who lived 3,500 years, the age of seven vultures.'

This accounts for the different ideas as regards the tradition of one Lokman in the preceding paragraph.

Before the era of the Prophet poetry had attained some degree of excellence. At the annual festival of Okatz the poets met and made public recitations, and competed for prizes. Of prose literature there was none, and the irregular, half-rhythmical, half-rhyming sentences of the Koran were the first attempts in the direction of prose.

Passing over the host of pre-Islamitic poets, the disputed time and order in which they appeared, as well as the ranks they respectively occupied, it will only be necessary here to describe the Arabic idyl or elegy (Kasida), and to notice the authors of the seven famous Mua'llakat, or suspended, or strung-together poems of the temple of Mecca, already alluded to above. As these poems were written in letters of gold, they were also called Muzahhibat, or 'gilded.' According to Arab notions, the subjects of a poet are four or five. He praises, loves, is angry, mourns, or describes either female beauty, animals, or objects of nature. Poems comprising one of these subjects only are short, but those treating of several are longer, and contain eulogies of chiefs, rulers, distinguished men and women, etc. The poet touches on the valour, liberality and eloquence of the hero, on the beauty and virtues of the woman, and describes the nearest surroundings, which are of the greatest interest, such as the horse, the camel, the antelope, the ostrich, the wild cow, the cloud, the lightning, wine, the vestiges of the tent of the beloved, and the hospitable camp-fire.

The Kasidas of the Mua'llakat are a series of smaller poems, composed on various occasions, and then strung together in one piece. Among them the two Kasidas of Amra-al-Kais (Amriolkais), and of Antara, are the most brilliant and romantic, on account of the sentiments of love they breathe towards the three beauties—Oneiza, Fatima, and Abla. The Kasida of Labid is famous for his description of both the camel and the horse; that of Tarafa for the delineation of the camel; that of Amru for the picture of a battle; while Harath chanted the praises of arms, and of the King of Hirah, and Zoheir produced a poem full of wise maxims. The whole seven contain a great deal about the personal feelings, the personal courage, the heroic deeds, and the wonderful adventures of the authors themselves—to which may be added descriptions of various animals, of hunting scenes, and of battle, the conventional lament for the absence or departure of a mistress, the delight of meeting her, and other bright sketches of Arab life in camp and on the march, with its joys, its sorrows, and its constant changes.

Sir William Jones first brought these poems to the notice of the West, and published a translation of them in A.D. 1782. 'They exhibit,' he says, 'an exact picture of the virtues and the vices, the wisdom and the folly, of the early Arabs. The poems show what may constantly be expected from men of open hearts and boiling passions, with no law to control, and little religion to restrain them.'

The above translations, with notes and remarks, have been reprinted by Mr. W. A. Clouston, in his 'Arabian Poetry for English Readers,' at Glasgow in 1881, and is a work well worthy of a perusal by any persons who may be interested in the subject.

The names of the three ancient Arab poets considered to have been possessed of equal talent with the authors of the Mua'llakat, are Nabiga, Al-Kama, and Al-Aasha, and some specimens of their composition, as also of those of other pre-Islamite poets, are to be found in the fifteenth volume, No. 39, pages 65-108, of the 'Bombay Branch of the Royal Asiatic Society,' translated by Mr. E. Rehatsek in 1881.

Second Period.

From Muhammad and his immediate successors (Abu Bakr, Omar, Othman and Ali), through the Omaiyide and Abbaside dynasties, to the end of the Khalifate of Baghdad, A.D. 1258.

The legislator of Islam, whose era began on the 16th July, A.D. 622 (though his actual departure from Mecca has been calculated to have taken place on the 20th June, A.D. 622), is here to be considered not from an historical, but from a poetical point of view. Although Muhammad despised the metres in which the bards of his nation chanted their Kasidas, and himself gave utterance in the name of Heaven to the inspirations of his genius only in richly-modulated and rhymed prose, nevertheless, according to the Oriental idea, he was regarded as a poet. Those who declare that he was not a poet overlook the circumstance that he was vehemently assailed by contemporary poets, who attempted to degrade his heaven-inspired Surahs into mere poetical fables. He himself protested against this insinuation, and declared at the end of the 26th Surah, entitled 'The Poets,' that those are in error who believe poets, as follows:

'And those who err follow the poets; dost thou not see how they roam (as bereft of their senses) through every valley (of the imagination) and that they say things which they do not perform? . . . Except those who believe, and do good works, and remember God frequently, and those who defend themselves after they have been unjustly treated by poets in their lampoons, and they who act unjustly shall know hereafter with what treatment they shall be treated.'

These lines are important as far as the history of literature is concerned. They are written against inimical poets, but distinguish the friendly ones, who, taking the part of Muhammad, repaid the lampooning poets in their own coin.

Some of the hostile poets, such as Hobeira and the woman Karitha, were killed at the taking of Mecca, whilst Zibary and the woman Hertlemah saved their lives only by making a profession of Islam. Muhammad had, however, also his panegyrists, the chief of whom was Ka'b bin Zoheir, the composer of the celebrated Kasida called 'The Poem of the Mantle,' as a reward for which the Prophet threw his own cloak over him, under the following circumstances, as related by Mr. J. W.

Redhouse in the preface to his translation of the poem published in the 'Arabian Poetry for English Readers'* alluded to above.

Ka'b was a son of Zoheir, already mentioned as the author of one of the pre-Islamite poems known as the 'Mua'llakat.' He had a brother named Bujeir, and, like their father, both brothers were good poets. Bujeir was first converted, and embraced the faith of Islam. Ka'b was angry at this, and composed a lampoon on his brother, on the Prophet, and on their new religion. This he sent to his brother by the mouth of a messenger. Bujeir repeated it to Muhammad, who commented on it as favourable to the new faith and to himself, but at the same time passed a sentence of death on the satirist.

Bujeir well knew that his brother's life was in danger, and warned him accordingly, advising him at the same time to renounce his errors, and come repentant to the Prophet, or to seek a safe asylum far away. Ka'b found out that his life would really soon be taken, and set out secretly for Madinah. There he found an old friend, claimed his protection, and went with him next morning to the simple meeting-house where Muhammad and his chief followers performed their daily devotions. When the service was ended, Ka'b approached

* In this same work will also be found a translation by Mr. Redhouse of another poem, also called 'The Poem of the Mantle,' but written by Sharaf-uddin Muhammad Al Busiri, who was born A.D. 1211, and died between A.D. 1291 and 1300.

Muhammad, and the two sat down together. Ka'b placed his own right hand in that of the Prophet, whom he addressed in these words: 'Apostle of God, were I to bring to you Ka'b, the son of Zoheir, penitent and professing the faith of Islam, wouldst thou receive and accept him?' The Prophet answered, 'I would.' 'Then,' said the poet, 'I am he!'

Hearing this, the bystanders demanded permission to put him to death. Muhammad ordered his zealous followers to desist, and the poet then, on the spur of the moment, recited a poem improvised at the time, probably with more or less premeditation. It is said that when Ka'b reached the fifty-first verse: 'Verily the Apostle of God is a light from which illumination is sought—a drawn Indian blade, one of the swords of God,' Muhammad took from his own shoulders the mantle he wore, and threw it over the shoulders of the poet as an honour and as a mark of protection. Hence the name given to the effusion, 'The Poem of the Mantle,' A.D. 630.

Moawia, the first Khalif of the Omaiyides, endeavoured to purchase this sacred mantle from Ka'b for ten thousand pieces of silver, but the offer was refused. Later on it was, however, bought from Ka'b's heirs for twenty thousand pieces of silver, and it passed into the hands of the Khalifs, and was preserved by them as one of the regalia of the empire until Baghdad was sacked by the

Mughals. The mantle, or what is supposed to be the self-same mantle, is now in the treasury* of the Sultan Khalif of the Ottomans at Constantinople, in an apartment named 'The Room of the Sacred Mantle,' in which this robe is religiously preserved, together with a few other relics of the great prophet.

Ka'b has thus come to be considered as one of the friendly poets, and the names of two others are also mentioned, viz., Abd-Allah bin Rewaha and Hassan bin Thabit. On the other hand, the most celebrated antagonists who attacked Muhammad, not only with their verses, but also with their swords, were Abu Sofyan, Amr bin Al-'A'asi, and Abd-Allah bin Zobeir. These three became great political characters, but later on made profession of Islam, and were the stanchest supporters of it, rendering the greatest services to the Prophet during his life, and to the cause after his death. But Muhammad's greatest triumph over the poets was the conversion of Labid, who, after the perusal of the commencement of the second Surah of the Koran, tore down his own poem, which was hung up in the Kaabah, and ran to the Prophet to

---

* *Apropos* of this treasury, it is much to be regretted that a complete catalogue of its contents has never been prepared along with a brief historical account of them. It is difficult to obtain the order, which comes direct from the Sultan, to visit the collection; and even then visitors are hurried through at such a pace that it is impossible to examine with minuteness the many curiosities collected there.

announce his conversion, and to make his profession of Islam. Even Ali, the cousin, son-in-law, and first convert of Muhammad, was a poet, but it is uncertain which of the Diwans attributed to him are genuine, and how many of his maxims of wisdom, over a hundred in number, are his own.

During the period under review the number of Arabic authors was legion. Some idea of the number of writers, and of the subjects on which they wrote, can be gathered from the Fihrist of An-Nadim, from Ibn Khallikan's Biographical Dictionary, and from Haji Khalfa's Encyclopædia. With such a mass of information as is contained in the above-mentioned works, it is difficult to deal in a small work. To put them together in an intelligible form, the idea of classing the authors, according to the subjects on which they principally wrote, naturally presented itself. This plan, therefore, has been followed, and a few details of the most celebrated writers will be given, classified under the following heads :

Jurisconsults.
Imams and lawyers.
Traditionists.
Alchemists.
Astronomers.
Grammarians.
Geographers and travellers.
Historians.

Lexicographers, biographers and encyclopædists.
Writers on natural history.
Philologists.
Philosophers.
Physicians.
Poets.
Collectors and editors of poems.
Translators.
The Omaiyide Khalifs.
The Abbaside Khalifs.
The Spanish Khalifs.

During the latter part of the first century of the Hijrah (July, 622—July, 719), the first persons of note in the Muhammadan world after Muhammad and his immediate successors were probably the seven jurisconsults, viz., Obaid Allah, Orwa, Kasim, Said, Sulaiman, Abu Bakr and Kharija, who all lived at Madinah about the same time; and it was from them, according to Ibn Khallikan, that the science of law and legal decisions spread over the world. They were designated by the appellation of the Seven Jurisconsults, because the right of giving decisions on points of law had passed to them from the companions of Muhammad, and they became publicly known as Muftis. These seven alone were acknowledged as competent to give Fatmas, or legal decisions. They died respectively A.D. 720, 712, 719, 710, 725, 712 and 718.

The jurisconsults were followed by the doctors of theology and law, or, as they were styled, Imams, or founders of the four orthodox sects. Now, among the Sunni Muslims an Imam may be described as a high-priest, or head, or chief in religious matters, whether he be the head of all Muhammadans—as the Khalifah—or the priest of a mosque, or the leader in the prayers of a congregation. This title, however, is given by the Shias only to the immediate descendants of Ali, the son-in-law of the Prophet, and they are twelve in number, Ali being the first. The last of them, Imam Mahdi, is supposed to be concealed (not dead), and the title which belongs to him cannot, they conceive, be given to another.

But among the Sunnis it is a dogma that there must always be a visible Imam or father of the Church. The title is given by them to the four learned doctors who were the exponents of their faith, viz., Imams Hanifa, Malik, Shafai and Hanbal. Of these, Imam Hanifa, the founder of the first of the four chief sects of the Sunnis, died A.D. 767. He was followed by Imam Malik, Imam Shafai, and Imam Hanbal, the founders of the other three sects, who died A.D. 795, 820 and 855 respectively. From these four persons are derived the various codes of Muhammadan jurisprudence. They have always been considered as the fundamental pillars of the orthodox law, and have been esteemed by Mussulmans as highly as the fathers of the Church—Gregory, Augustine, Jerome and Chrysostom—have been appreciated by Christians.

Of these four sects, the Hanbalite and Malikite may be considered as the most rigid, the Shafaite as the most conformable to the spirit of Islamism, and the Hanifite as the wildest and most philosophical of them all.

In addition to the four Imams just mentioned, there was a fifth, of the name of Abu Sulaiman Dawud az Zahari, who died A.D. 883. He was the founder of the sect called Az-Zahariah (the External), and his lectures were attended by four hundred Fakihs (doctors of the civil and of the ecclesiastical law), who wore shawls thrown over their shoulders. But his opinions do not seem to have secured many followers, and in time both his ideas, and those of Sofyan at Thauri, another chief of the orthodox sect, were totally abandoned.

The third century of the Hijrah (A.D. 816-913) is noted for the six fathers of tradition, viz., Al-Bukhari, Muslim, At Firmidi, Abu Dawud, An-Nasai and Ibn Majah, with whom others, such as Kasim bin Asbagh, Abu Zaid, Al-Marwazi, Abu Awana and Al-Hazini, vied in great works on tradition, but these last-named could never acquire the authority of the six previously mentioned, who died A.D. 870, 875, 892, 889, 916, 887 respectively.

In the beginning of Islam the great traditionists were Ayesha, the favourite wife of the Prophet, the four rightly directed Khalifs, viz., Abu Bakr, Omar, Othman and Ali, and some of the companions* known as the Evangelists of Islam. But besides these well-qualified persons who had lived with or near Muhammad during his lifetime, many others who had perhaps only seen him or spoken to him claimed to be considered as companions, who handed down traditions ; and when these were all dead they were followed by others, who, having known the companions, were now designated as the successors of the companions.

Under these circumstances it can easily be imagined that many of the traditions were of doubtful authenticity. Al-Bukhari, whose collection of traditions of the Muhammadan religion holds the first place, both as regards authority and correctness, selected seven thousand two hundred and seventy-five of the most authentic out of ten thousand, all of which he regarded as being true, having rejected two hundred thousand as false. His book is held in the highest estimation, and considered both in spiritual and temporal matters as next in authority to the Koran. He was born A.D. 810, and died A.D. 870.

The Shiahs do not accept the collection of

---

* The names of these companions, and the kings, princes, and countries to which they were sent by Muhammad, are given in full detail in 'The Life of our Lord Muhammad, the Apostle of God,' the author of which was Ibn Ishak; and it was afterwards edited by Ibn Hisham. In the same work a list is given of the disciples sent out by Jesus.

traditions as made by the Sunnis, but have a collection of their own, upon which their system of law, both civil and religious, is founded.

During the first and second centuries of the Hijrah (A.D. 622-816), of all the physical sciences alchemy was studied most. The greatest scientific man of the first century was undoubtedly Khalid, a prince of the Omaiyide dynasty, and the son of Yazid I. His zeal for knowledge and science induced him to get Greek and Syriac works translated by Stephanus into Arabic, especially those which treated on chemistry, or rather alchemy. Khalid, having been once reproached for wasting all his time in researches in the art of alchemy, replied: 'I have occupied myself with these investigations to show my contemporaries and brothers that I have found in them a recompense and a reward for the Khalifate which I lost. I stand in need of no man to recognise me at court, and I need not recognise anyone who dances attendance at the portals of dominion either from fear, ambition, or covetousness.' He wrote a poem on alchemy, which bears the title of 'Paradise of Wisdom,' and of him Ibn Khallikan says: 'He was the most learned man of the tribe of Koraish in all the different branches of knowledge. He wrote a discourse on chemistry and on medicine, in which sciences he possessed great skill and solid information.' He died A.D. 704.

Later on Jaber bin Hayam, with his pupils,

became a model for later alchemists, and he has been called the father of Arabian chemistry. He compiled a work of two thousand pages, in which he inserted the problems of his master, Jaafar as Sadik, considered to be the father of all the occult sciences in Islam. Jaber was such a prolific writer that many of his five hundred works are said to bear his name only on account of his celebrity, but to have been written in reality by a variety of authors. His works on alchemy were published in Latin by Golius, under the title of 'Lapis Philosophorum,' and an English translation of them by Robert Russell appeared at Leyden in A.D. 1668. Jaber died A.D. 766, and is not to be confounded with Al-Jaber (Geber), the astronomer, who lived at Seville about A.D. 1190, and constructed there an astronomical observatory.

Astronomy appears to have been always a favourite science with the Arabs from the earliest times. In A.D. 772 there appeared at the court of the Khalif Mansur (A.D. 754-775), Muhammad bin Ibrahim bin Habib al Fezari, the astronomer, who brought with him the tables called Sind Hind, in which the motions of the stars were calculated according to degrees. They contained other observations on solar eclipses and the rising of the signs of the zodiac, extracted by him from the tables ascribed to the Indian king, Figar. The Khalif Mansur ordered this book to be translated into Arabic to serve as a guide for Arab astronomers. And these tables remained in use till the time of the Khalif Mamun (A.D. 813-833), when other revised ones bearing his name came into vogue. These, again, were abridged by Abul Ma'shar (Albumasar, died A.D. 885-886), called the prince of Arabian astrologers, who, however, deviated from them, and inclined towards the system of the Persians and of Ptolemy. This second revision was more favourably received by the Arab astronomers than the first, and the Sind Hind was superseded by the Almagest of Ptolemy. Better astronomical instruments also came into use, though previously the Al-Fezari above mentioned had been the first in Islam who constructed astrolabes of various kinds, and had written several astronomical treatises.

Mention might be made of about forty mathematicians and astronomers who wrote books on these subjects. The best of them, such as Al-Farghani (Alfraganius) and others, lived at the court of Mamun, who built an astronomical observatory in Baghdad and another near Damascus, on Mount Kasiun. He caused also two degrees of the meridian to be measured on the plain of Sinjar, so as to ascertain the circumference of the earth with more precision. In A.D. 824 there were held philosophical disputations in his presence. Al-Farghani was the author of an introduction to astronomy, which was printed by Golius at Amsterdam in 1669, with notes.

Between the years A.D. 877 and 929 there flourished the famous calculator and astronomer, Muhammad bin Jaber al Battani, Latinized as Albategnius. He was the author of the astronomical work entitled 'The Sabæan Tables,' and adopted nearly the system and the hypothesis of Ptolemy, but rectified them in several points, and made other discoveries, which procured him a distinguished place among the scholars whose labours have enriched astronomical science. Al-Battani approached much nearer to the truth than the ancients as far as the movements of the fixed stars are concerned. He measured the greatness of the eccentricity of the solar orbit, and a more correct result cannot be obtained. To the work containing all his discoveries he gave the name of 'As-Zij-as Sabi,' which was translated into Latin under the title 'De Scientiâ Stellarum.' The first edition of it appeared at Nuremberg in A.D. 1537, but it is believed that the original work is in the library of the Vatican. He was classed by Lalande among the forty-two most celebrated astronomers of the world. He died A.D. 929-930.

Another celebrated astronomer, Ali bin Yunis, was a native of Egypt, and appears to have lived at the court of the demented tyrant of Egypt, Al-Hakim bramrillah, and under his patronage to have composed the celebrated astronomical tables called, after his name, 'The Hakimite Tables.' Ibn Khallikan states that he had seen these tables in four volumes, and that more extensive ones had not come under his notice. These tables were considered in Egypt to be of equal value to those of the astronomer Yabya bin Ali Mansur, who had in A.D. 830, by order of the Khalif Mamun, undertaken astronomical observations both at Baghdad and Damascus. Ibn Yunis spent his life in the preparation of astronomical tables and in casting horoscopes, for it must be remembered that with the Muslims astronomy and astrology were synonymous, and their most learned astronomers were also their most skilful astrologers. His character for honesty was highly esteemed, and he was also well versed in other sciences, and displayed an eminent talent for poetry. He died A.D. 1009, and is not to be confounded with his father, Ibn Yunis, the historian, who died A.D. 958.

Yet another name must be mentioned, viz., the Spanish-Arab astronomer Ibn Abd-ar-rahman es-Zerkel, Europeanized as Arzachal. He first resided at Toledo, at the court of its sovereign, Mamun, for whom he made an astrolabe, which he called in his honour the Mamunian. He then went to Seville, where he wrote for Motamid bin Abbad (A.D. 1069-1091) a treatise on the use of certain instruments. During his residence at Toledo he constructed two clepsydras, the waters of which decreased and increased according to the waning and growing of the moon, and these two basins were destroyed only in A.D. 1133 by Alphonse VI., when he took

Toledo. Arzachal left a work on eclipses, and on the revolution of years, as well as the tables of the sky, to which the name of Toledan tables have been given. His writings, but especially the last, which must have been consulted by the editors of the Alphonsine tables, were never translated, and exist only in manuscript in libraries where but few scholars can consult them. Arzachal made many observations in connection with the sun, and was also the inventor of the astronomical instrument called after his name, Zerkalla. He died A.D. 1080.

Before leaving this subject it may be mentioned that Makkari, in his great encyclopædia of Spain, enumerates fifteen astronomers of Andalusia, all more or less known in their time. Also that Bedei-ul-Astrolabi and Ibn Abdul-Rayman distinguished themselves as makers of astronomical instruments, and inventors of new ones. While Arzachal was the greatest representative of Arab astronomy in the West, Umar Khayam, the astronomer, mathematician, freethinker, and poet, was its greatest representative in the East, in Persia, where he died A.D. 1123.

A great deal in Arabic literature has been written about grammar, and, until its principles were finally laid down and established, it was always a source of continual controversy between different professors and different schools. Abul Aswad ad-Duwali has been called the father of

Arabic grammar. It is said that the Khalif Ali laid down for him this principle: the parts of speech are three, the noun, the verb, and the particle, and told him to form a complete treatise upon it. This was accordingly done: and other works on the subject were also produced, but none of them are apparently now extant. Muhammad bin Ishak has stated that he saw one of them, entitled 'Discourse on the Governing and the Governed Parts of Speech;' and the author of the 'Fihrist' also alludes to this work. Abul-Aswad died at Busra in A.D. 688, aged eighty-five, but some years later his two successors in this branch of literature (viz., Al-Khalil and Sibawaih) far surpassed him in every way.

Al-Khalil bin Ahmad, born A.D. 718, was one of the great masters in the science of grammar, and the discoverer of the rules of prosody, which art owes to him its creation. He laid the foundation of the language by his book 'Al-Ain' (so called from the letter with which it begins), and by the aid he afforded thereby to Sibawaih, whose master he was, in the composition of his celebrated grammatical work known by the name of 'The Book.' In the work called 'Al-Ain,' Khalil first arranged the stock of Arabic words, dealing with the organ of speech and the production of sounds, and then dividing the words into classes, the roots of which consisted of one, two, three, four, or five letters. It is still a matter of dispute whether the book

'Al-Ain' was wholly composed by Khalil himself, or completed in course of time by his pupils. A copy of this celebrated lexicon and work on philology is in the Escurial Library. Khalil also wrote a treatise on prosody, and other works on grammar, and a book on musical intonation. He died A.D. 786, at Busra. 'Poverty,' he said, 'consists not in the want of money, but of soul; and riches are in the mind, not in the purse.'

Sibawaih, the pupil of Khalil, has been called the father of Arabic lexicography, and the law-giver of Arabic grammar. Ibn Khallikan says that he was a learned grammarian, and surpassed in this science every person of former and later times. As for his 'Kitab,' or 'Book,' composed by him on that subject, it has never had its equal. The great philologist and grammarian, Al-Jahiz, said of the book of Sibawaih, that none like it had ever been written on grammar, and that all writers on this subject who had succeeded him had borrowed from it. When Al-Kisai was tutor to the prince Al-Amin, son of Harun-ar-Rashid, Sibawaih came to Baghdad, and the two great grammarians (Sibawaih, the chief of the school of Busra, and Al-Kisai, chief of the school of Kufa) had a long dispute about a certain expression of Arabic speech, and an Arab of the desert was called in to arbitrate between them. The man first decided in favour of Sibawaih, but when the question was put in another form, the Bedouin asserted that Kisai was right.

As Sibawaih considered that he had been unjustly treated in the matter, he left Baghdad for good. The year of his death has been given differently by various authors, the earliest date being A.D. 787, and the latest A.D. 809.

The most celebrated grammarians of the third century of the Hijrah (A.D. 816 - 913) were Al-Mubarrad, who died A.D. 898, and Thalab, who died A.D. 903. They were also great antagonists to each other. Al-Mubarrad, the author of thirty works, was the chief of the school of Busra, and Thalab of that of Kufa, both founded during the preceding century by Sibawaih and Kisai. Thalab was the first collector of books in Islam, and those left by him were very valuable.

Mention must also be made of Al-Farra, the grammarian, and distinguished by his knowledge of grammar, philology, and various branches of literature. He died A.D. 822, at the age of sixty-three, and preceded both Mubarrad and Thalab, the latter of whom used to say: 'Were it not for Al-Farra, pure Arabic would no longer exist; it was he who disengaged it from the ordinary language and fixed it by writing.' At the request of the Khalif Al-Mamun he drew up in two years a most elaborate work, which contained the principles of grammar, and all the pure Arabic expressions which he had heard. It was entitled 'Al-Hudúd' (the Limits or Chapters), and directly it was finished he commenced another in connection with the Koran, which is spoken of as a most wonderful production. He wrote besides several other works on grammar, and acted as tutor to the two sons of the Khalif Mamun.

Though many other grammarians could be named, such as Al-Akhfash al Ausat, Abu Amr as Shaibani, Abu Bakr al Anbari, etc., none can be considered so celebrated as the persons above mentioned, who are regarded as the founders of the principles on which Arabic grammar has been established.

In the middle of the third century of the Hijrah (A.D. 816-913), the Arabs first began to distinguish themselves as travellers and geographers. When Muslim Homeir was, in A.D. 845, ransomed from his captivity among the Byzantines and returned to his country, he wrote a book with the title of 'Admonitions on the Countries, Kings and Offices of the Greeks.' Forty years afterwards Jaafar bin Ahmed al Mervezi produced the first geographical work under the title of 'Highways and Countries,' which was followed by those of Ibn Foslan, Ibn Khordabeh, Jeihani, Al-Istakhri, Ibn Haukul, Al-Beruni, Al-Bekri and Idrisi. The great historian, Masudi, was also a writer of travels and an ambassador. Ibn Foslan was sent by the Khalif Muktadir (A.D. 908-932) to the King of the Bulgarians. Abu Dolaf, who accompanied an ambassador from China to the frontiers of that country, made, on his return, a report which Yakut afterwards embodied in his voluminous geographical Dictionary.

A few details will be given about the six chief geographers and travellers of this period, viz., Ibn Khordabeh, Al-Istakhri, Ibn Haukul, Al-Beruni, Al-Bekri and Idrisi.

As regards the first-named, it would appear that he has been the object of considerable controversies among the Orientalists of Europe. After employment in the post and intelligence departments in the provinces, he subsequently came to the court of the Khalif Motamid (A.D. 870-892), and became one of his privy councillors. He is the author of several works on various subjects, but his 'Geography,' says Sir H. M. Elliot, is the only work we possess of this author, and of this there is only one copy in Europe, in the Bodleian Library at Oxford. He died about A.D. 912.

Al-Istakhri, who flourished about the year A.D. 951, obtained his name from Istakhar (i.e., Persepolis), where he was born. He was a traveller whose geographical work has been translated into German by Mordtmann. When Istakhari was in the Indus Valley he met another celebrated traveller, Ibn Haukul, whose book Sir William Ouseley translated in A.D. 1800 into English, under the title of 'The Oriental Geography of Ibn Haukul.' Haukul, who died A.D. 976, had travelled for nearly twenty-eight years in the countries of Islam with the works of Ibn

Khordabeh and Jeihani in his hands, and his work, which bears the generally approved title of 'Highways and Countries,' is based on the book of Istakhri.

But the greatest geographer and naturalist of this period is Abu Raihan Al-Beruni (born about A.D. 971), who accompanied Mahmud the Ghaznavide on his invasions to India. He was to Mahmud of Ghazni what Aristotle was to Alexander, with the difference, however, that he actually accompanied the conqueror on his Indian campaigns. He travelled into different countries and to and from India for the space of forty years, and during that time was much occupied with astronomy and astronomical observations, as well as geography. His works are said to have exceeded a camel-load, but the most valuable of all of them is his description of India. It gives an account of the religion of India, its philosophy, literature, geography, chronology, astronomy, customs, law and astrology about A.D. 1030, and has been edited by Edward Sachau, Professor in the Royal University of Berlin. An English edition, containing a preface, the translation of the Arabic text, notes and indices, has also been published. Al-Beruni died at Ghurna A.D. 1038. He used to correspond with Avicenna, who was his contemporary, and who gives in his works the answers to the questions addressed to him by this famous geographer, astronomer, geometrician, historian, scholar, and logician.

Some years later Abu O'beid Abd-Allah Al-Bekri distinguished himself as one of the greatest geographers, with whose labours Quatremere and Dozy and Gayangos have made us better acquainted. He was, by birth, from Andalusia, whence also many others travelled to the East, either for instruction or for trade or as pilgrims, and of whom about a couple of dozen are mentioned by Makkari. Some of these gave descriptions and topographies, to which class of literature also the poetical laudations of celebrated towns belong. Not only Baghdad, Damascus, Cairo, Fez, Morocco and Khairwan were praised or satirized, but also Cordova, Seville, Granada, Malaga, Toledo, Valencia and Zohra were described in Arabic poems. Al-Bekri died in A.D. 1094-1095, and was followed by Idrisi, the author of a work on Arabian geography of some celebrity, and which has been translated into Latin. He died A.D. 1164.

Of historians in Arab literature there are many, but only the most celebrated will be noted. Muhammad bin Ishak, who died about A.D. 767, produced the best and most trustworthy biography of the prophet Muhammad. His work was published under the patronage of the Abbaside princes, and was, in fact, composed for the Khalif Al-Mansur (A.D. 754-775). It was used as the chief source of information by Ibn Hisham, the next historian of note, in his life of the Prophet, which work has been edited by Dr. Wüstenfeld, and translated into German by Dr. Weil, and into English by Mr. E. Rehatsek, whose manuscript, however, has not yet been printed. Ibn Hisham, who died in A.D. 828, was the father of Arabic genealogy, and Abu-el-Siyadi, who died in A.D. 857, is next to him.

But the real father of Arabian history was Al-Wackidi, a good and trustworthy historian, thirty-two of whose works are known, all relating to the conquests of the Arabs, and other such subjects. He died A.D. 822. With him generally has been associated his secretary, Muhammad bin Saad, a man of unimpeachable integrity, and of the highest talents, merit, and eminence. He has left us some most interesting works, full of valuable information relating to those times. He died at Baghdad A.D. 844.

Al-Madaini, who died A.D. 839, was the author of two hundred and fifty historical works, of which, however, nothing has yet been discovered, except their titles as given in the 'Fihrist.'

Passing over many other historians, two more only will be mentioned, viz., Abu Jafir at-Tabari and Al-Masúdi.

Tabari (whose annals are now being edited by a company of European Orientalists) was born A.D. 838, at Amol, in the province of Tabaristan. He travelled a great deal, and composed many works on history, poetry, grammar and lexicography. His work on jurisprudence extends to several volumes, and his historical works stamp him as one of the most reliable of Arab historians, while his numerous other works also bear witness to the variety and accuracy of his acquirements. He died at Baghdad A.D. 923, and has been called by Gibbon the Livy of the Arabians.

Al-Masúdi, a contemporary of the great historian Tabari, died thirty-four years after him, in A.D. 957. His great work, 'Meadows of Gold and Mines of Gems,' with the Arabic text above and a French translation below, has been published in nine volumes (1861-1877) by Barbier de Meynard, in connection with Pavet de Courteille, at the expense of the French Government. Dr. A. Sprenger (who translated one volume of the work into English for the Oriental Translation Fund, London, 1841) calls the author of it the Herodotus of Arabian history, because he had, like his Greek prototype, undertaken extensive travels, and had like him made the description of countries and nations his chief occupation. The titles of ten of his works are known to us, but the principal one is that named above, in the composition of which he used eighty-five historical, geographical, and philological works, as he himself informs us in the first chapter of his history. The work itself contains one hundred and thirty-two chapters.

Ibn al Athir al Jazari, born A.D. 1160 and died A.D. 1233, was also an historian of note, and a personal friend of Ibn Khallikan, who writes of him as follows : 'His knowledge of the Traditions, and his acquaintance with that science in its various branches, placed him in the first rank; and his learning as an historian of the ancients and moderns was not less extensive; he was perfectly familiar with the genealogy of the Arabs, their adventures, combats and history: whilst his great work, " The Kâmil or Complete," embracing the history of the world from the earliest period to the year 628 of the Hijrah (A.D. 1230-1231), merits its reputation as one of the best productions of the kind.' Another of Ibn Al Athir's works is the history of the most eminent among the companions of Muhammad, in the shape of a biographical dictionary.

As the development of Arab letters proceeded, in the course of time various authors began to tabulate the different branches of knowledge and science, and these, with the biographies of many of the writers, and the lists of their works, formed a distinct branch in the literature of that day.

The most noteworthy of them all was Abul Faraj Muhammad bin Ishak, who is generally known by the name of Ibn Ali Yakub al Warrak the copyist, surnamed An-Nadim al Baghdadi, the social companion from Baghdad, and the author of the 'Fihrist.' It may be truly said that this writer, along with Ibn Khallikan, laid the foundations of the records of the edifice of encyclopædical and biographical works, which was afterwards completed by Haji Khalfa and Abul Khair. Without the work of Ibn Khallikan it would be as impossible to give a history of Arab scholars, as without the work of An-Nadim to give an account of Arab literature.

The 'Kitab al-Fihrist' was written by An-Nadim in A.D. 987, and is divided into ten sections, dealing with every branch of letters and learning. It gives the names of many authors and their works long since extant, and shows the enormous amount of writings produced by the Arabs during the periods under review, up to A.D. 987, the date of the author's work. A short account of this ancient and curious book has been given in the *Journal Asiatique* for December, 1839, and from the work itself Von Hammer Purgstall has been able to gather that the 'Thousand and One Nights' ('Arabian Nights') had a Persian origin. In the eighth section of the 'Fihrist' the author says that the first who composed tales and apologues were the kings of the early Persian dynasties, and that these tales were augmented and amplified by the Sasanians (A.D. 228-641). The Arabs then translated them into their own language, and composed other stories like them.

Ibn Khallikan, the most worthy of biographers, must also be mentioned here, though he died in A.D. 1282, twenty-four years after the fall of Baghdad, having been born in A.D. 1211. This very eminent scholar and follower of Shafa'i doctrines, was born at Arbela, but resided at

Damascus, where he had filled the place of Chief Kadi till the year A.D. 1281, when he was dismissed, and from that time to the day of his death he never went out of doors. He was a man with the greatest reputation for learning, versed in various sciences, and highly accomplished. He was a scholar, a poet, a compiler, a biographer and an historian. By his talents and writings he merited the honourable title of the most learned man and the ablest historian. His celebrated biographical work, called the 'Wafiat-ul-Aiyan,' or Deaths of Eminent Men, is the acme of perfection. This work was translated from the Arabic by Baron MacGuckin de Slane, a member of the council of the Asiatic Society of Paris, and printed by the Oriental Translation Fund of Great Britain and Ireland in A.D. 1842, 1843, 1868 and 1871. For all those who wish to gain a knowledge of the legal literature of the Muhammadans it is a most valuable work, as the Baron has added to the text numerous learned notes, replete with curious and interesting information relating to the Muhammadan law and lawyers. Ibn Khallikan died, aged seventy-three lunar years, in the Najibia College at Damascus, and was buried in the cemetery of As-Salihiya, a well-known village situated on the declivity of Mount Kasiun, a short distance to the north of Damascus, and from which a splendid view of the town and its surrounding gardens is obtained. When lately there I made inquiries about the tomb of this great Arab *littérateur*, but without success. His tomb has quite disappeared, and his name seemed to be forgotten; but his work still lives, an everlasting monument of his industry and his intelligence.

It will be remembered that the early Arab poets described men, women, animals, and their surroundings in their effusive Kasidas before prose-writing was established. Later on grammarians and philologists began to write books on the different objects of nature and on the physiology of man; also treatises on the horse, the camel, bees, mountains, seas, rivers, and all natural phenomena. There were thus laid down, though not a scientific, at least a philological basis, for the future development of the natural sciences and geography. Such monographs were only in later times collected in encyclopædic works, in which they were inserted in such a manner as to constitute various chapters only, and no longer separate treatises.

Khalef-al-Ahmer (whom Suyuti declared to be a great forger, because he pretended that some poems written by himself had been composed by ancient Arab poets) wrote the first book on Arab mountains, and about the poems recited concerning them. Ahmed bin-ud Dinveri wrote, in addition to several grammatical and mathematical works, a book on plants, and after him the grammarian Al-Jahiz wrote the first treatise on animals, but more from a philological point of view than from that of natural history. He wrote, moreover, on theology, geography, natural history, and philology; but his most celebrated work is his 'Book of Animals,' in which he displayed all his knowledge of the Arabic tongue. He was frightfully ugly, and obtained the surname of Jahiz on account of his protuberant eyes. He himself informs us that the Khalif Mutwakkil intended to appoint him as tutor to his sons, but was deterred by his ugliness, and dismissed him with a present of ten thousand dirhems. Al-Jahiz died A.D. 869, over ninety years of age.

Philology is a term now generally used as applicable to that science which embraces human language in its widest extent, and may be shortly called 'the science of language.' But in earlier times philology included, with few exceptions, everything that could be learned—many and various subjects, without particular reference to the meaning now generally adopted concerning it.

There will be found among the Arab authors of this period many philologists who also wrote upon other matters, but have been recorded here as having particularly excelled in this particular branch of learning.

Al Kasim bin Ma'an was the first who wrote on the rarities of the language and on the peculiarities of authors, and, according to the 'Fihrist,' he surpassed all his contemporaries by the variety of his information. Tradition and traditionists, poetry and poets, history and historians, scholastic theology and theologians, genealogy and genealogists, were the subjects on which he displayed the extent of his acquirements. He died A.D. 791.

Abu Ali Muhammad bin-al Mustanir bin Ahmad, generally known by the name of Kutrub, was also a grammarian and philologist, and wrote books and treatises on these subjects, as also on natural history. He died A.D. 821.

Philology and Arabic poetry were the special objects of the studies of Abu Amr Ishak bin Mirar as Shaibani, and in these two branches of knowledge his authority is of the highest order. He composed a number of works and treatises, and wrote with his own hand upwards of eighty volumes. He died A.D. 825.

But the two earliest, and perhaps the two most celebrated, philologists were Al-Asmai and Abu Obaida, who outshone their successors for all time to come, and were distinguished—the former by his wit, and the latter by his scholarship.

Abu Said Abd-al Malik bin Kuraib al-Asmai was born A.D. 739 or 740, and died A.D. 831. He was a complete master of the Arabic language, an able grammarian, and the most eminent of all those who transmitted orally historical narrations, anecdotes, stories, and rare expressions of the language. When the poet Abu Nuwas was informed that Asmai and Abu Obaida had been introduced at Harun's court, he said that the latter would narrate ancient and modern history, but that the former would charm with his melodies. Ibn Shabba was informed by Asmai himself 'that he knew by heart sixteen thousand pieces of verse composed in the measure called Rajaz, or free metre,' and Ishak al Mausili asserted 'that he never heard al-Asmai profess to know a branch of science without discovering that none knew it better than he.' No one ever explained better than Al-Asmai the idioms of the desert Arabs. Most of his works, which amount to thirty-six, treat of the language and its grammar; but he also wrote a book on the horse and different treatises on various other animals, such as the camel, the sheep, wild beasts, etc., and their physiology.

Al-Asmai's contemporary, Abu Obaida, was an able grammarian and an accomplished scholar. He was born A.D. 728, and died at Busra A.D. 824, leaving nearly two hundred treatises, of which the names of many have been given by Ibn Khallikan, and most of them are of a purely philological character. There are many anecdotes about him, and many sayings of clever men regarding him. Abu Nuwas took lessons from Abu Obaida, praised him highly, and decried Al-Asmai, whom he detested. When asked what he thought of Al-Asmai, he replied, 'A nightingale in a cage,' meaning probably that a nightingale in a cage is pleasing to hear, but there is nothing else good about it. Abu Obaida he described as 'a bundle of science packed up in a skin.'

Abu Zaid al-Ansari was a philologist and grammarian, and a contemporary of the two persons just described. He held the first rank among the literary men of that time, and devoted his attention principally to the study of the philology of the Arabic language, its singular terms and rare expressions. Of him Al-Mubarrad said : ' Abu Zaid was an abler grammarian than Al-Asmai and Abu Obaida, but these two came next to him, and were near to each other. Abu Obaida was the most accomplished scholar of the day.' Abu Zaid composed a number of useful philological works, and titles of thirty-one of them are given in the 'Fihrist.' He died A.D. 830, over ninety years of age.

Abu Othman Bakr bin Muhammad bin Habib al-Mayini, briefly called Abu Othman, was celebrated as a philologer and grammarian, as also for his knowledge in general literature. He learned philology from Abu Zaid, Abu Obaida, Al-Asmai, and others, and had for pupil Al-Mubarrad, who learned much from his master, and handed down many pieces of traditional literature obtained from him. Abu Othman, once being asked his opinion about various men of science, curtly summarized them as follows : 'The Koran readers are deceitful administrators, the traditionists are satisfied with superfluities, poets are too superficial, grammarians much too heavy, narrators deal only in neat expressions, and the only real science is jurisprudence.' He died A.D. 863.

Abul Aina was a philologist, but also a great joker, anecdote-teller, and poet. His memory was equal to his eloquence, and, being quick-witted, he was never in want of a repartee when the occasion required it; indeed, he ranked among the most brilliant wits of the age. To a vizier, who said that everything current about the liberality of the Barmekides was only so much exaggeration and invention of leaf-scribblers, he replied: 'Of you, O vizier, the leaf-scribblers will certainly report nothing and invent nothing.' There are many other anecdotes and stories told about him. Being asked how long he would continue to praise some and satirize others, he replied: 'As long as the virtuous do good and the wicked do evil, but God forbid that I should be as the scorpion which stingeth equally the prophet and the infidel.' He had a most wonderful memory, which he applied, however, not to the preservation of interpretations and their vouchers, but to that of anecdotes, drolleries, and witty sayings, wherefore his name has been perpetuated as that of a joker. He died A.D. 896.

Mention must also be made of Abdullah bin Muslim bin Kutaiba, who was a philologist and grammarian of eminent talent, and noted for the correctness of his information. He was the author of many works, such as 'The Book of Facts,' 'The Writer's Guide,' 'Notices on the Poets,' and 'A Treatise on Horses,' and others, all of which were more or less celebrated in their time. He was born A.D. 828, and died, some say, in A.D. 884, others in A.D. 908.

Ibn Duraid, whose many other names are given by Ibn Khallikan, is described by that author as 'the most accomplished scholar, the ablest philologer, and the first poet of the age.' Masudi and other men of learning also speak of him in the highest terms. He composed several works on natural history, and produced also a complete Dictionary of this kind, after the model of the books 'Al-A'in' and 'Al-Jim,' the two letters of the alphabet with which Khalil, the grammarian, and Abu Amr as Shaibani respectively began their works. Ibn Duraid died at Baghdad A.D. 933. The celebrated Motazelite divine Abu Haslim Abd-as Salam al-Jubbai died the same day, and this caused the people to say that 'To-day philology and dogmatic theology have ceased to exist.'

In the East, by philosophy not only logic and metaphysics are meant, but also all ethical, political, mathematical, and medical sciences. Indeed, it may be said that nearly all learned men were in those days called philosophers, a term which included mathematicians, astronomers, physicians, encyclopaedists and others.

From the mass of Arab authors all laying claim

to the title of philosopher, it is perhaps an invidious task to select a few only, and even those selected by one person might be rejected by another. But public opinion will probably agree in naming three persons as having claim to the highest rank in Arab learning. They are Al-Kindi, Al-Farabi, and Ali-ibn Sina, commonly called Avicenna. Ali-bin Ridhwan, Al-Ghazali, Ibn Bajah (Avempace), and Ibn Rashid (Averroes) have also their claims to be considered, while Thalab bin Korra, Kosta bin Luka, Al-Tavhidi, and Al-Majridi were also all eminent men. A few details will be given about the first seven of the names just mentioned.

Yakub-bin Ishak Al-Kindi, the philosopher of the Arabs, known in Europe by the corrupted name of Alchendius, possessed an encyclopædic mind, and being himself a living encyclopædia, he composed one of all the sciences. He divided philosophy into three branches, the mathematical, the physical, and the ethical. He declared the nullity of alchemy, which Ibn Sina had again brought to honourable notice, till the physician Abdul Latif declaimed against it. But Al-Kindi was not sufficiently advanced to write against astrology, which is still in full force all over the East even in our own times. Only one of his works has as yet been published in Europe, and that treats on the composition of medicines, though we possess the titles of not less than two hundred and thirty-four works composed by him on a variety of subjects. He died A.D. 861.

Abu Nasr Al-Farabi (Alfarabius), called by the Arabs a second Aristotle, is generally considered to be the second Arab philosopher; Avicenna, who always quotes him in his works, the third; the first place being assigned to Al-Kindi. Al-Farabi studied Arabic (he was a Turk by birth) and philosophy in Baghdad, where he attended the lectures of Abu Bishr Matta bin Yunus, who possessed, and also imparted to his pupils, the gift of expressing the deepest meanings in the easiest words. From Baghdad he went to Harran, where Yuhanna bin Khailan, the Christian philosopher, was teaching logic, and after his return he made all the works of Aristotle his special study. It is related that the following note was found inscribed in Al-Farabi's handwriting on a copy of Aristotle's treatise on the soul: 'I have read over this book two hundred times.' He also said that he had read over Aristotle's 'Physics' forty times, and felt that he ought to read it over again. Abul Kasim Said, of Cordova, says in his 'Classes of Philosophers' that 'Al-Farabi led all the professors of Islam to the right understanding of logic by unveiling and explaining its secrets, as well as by considering all those points which Al-Kindi had neglected, and by teaching the application of analogy to all occurring cases.' In his enumeration and limitation of the sciences, Al-Farabi embraced the whole system of knowledge as it then existed. He went to Egypt, and afterwards to Damascus, where he died in A.D. 950. During his residence at Damascus he was mostly to be found near the borders of some rivulet, or in a shady garden; there he composed his works and received the visits of his pupils. He was extremely abstemious, and entirely indifferent to wealth and poverty. The list of his works on philosophical and scientific subjects amount to sixty-one. Mr. Munk's 'Mélanges de Philosophie Juive et Arabe' (Paris, 1859) contains good articles on Al-Farabi and Al-Kindi.

Ibn Sina (Avicenna) was a great philosopher and physician. At the age of ten years he had completed the study of the Koran in Bukhara, where afterwards a certain Natili became his tutor, with whom he first studied the 'Eisagoge' of Porphyry, and afterwards Euclid, and lastly the 'Almagest' of Ptolemy. Natili then departed, and an ardent desire to study medicine having taken possession of Ibn Sina, he commenced to read medical books, which not being so difficult to understand as mathematics and metaphysics, he made such rapid progress in them that he soon became an excellent physician, and cured his patients by treating them with well-approved remedies. He began also to study jurisprudence before he was thirteen. At the age of eighteen he entered the service of a prince of the Beni

Saman dynasty, Nuh bin Mansur, at Bukhara, a paralytic, who entertained many physicians at his court, and Ibn Sina joined their number. There he composed his 'Collection,' in which he treated of all the sciences except mathematics, and there also he wrote his book of 'The Acquirer and the Acquired.' He then left Bukhara, and lived in various towns of Khurasan, but never went further west, spending his whole life in the countries beyond the Oxus, in Khwarizm and in Persia, although he wrote in Arabic. It would be superfluous to follow all his changes of fortune, but it may be mentioned that when he was the first physician and vizier of Mezd-ud-daulah, a sultan of the Bowide dynasty, he was twice deposed and put in irons. He also appears to have acted treacherously towards Ala-ud-daulah, a prince of Ispahan, who was his benefactor. He was four years in prison, but at last succeeded in deceiving his guardians, and escaped. His dangerous travels, and the depression of mind inseparable from reverses of fortune, however, never interrupted his scientific pursuits. His taste for study and his activity were such that, as he himself informs us, not a single day passed in which he had not written fifty leaflets. The list of manuscripts left by him, and scattered in various libraries of Europe, is considerable, and though many of his works have been lost, some are still in existence. The fatigues of his long journeys, and the excesses of all kinds in which he indulged, abridged the life of this celebrated scholar, who died in A.D. 1037, at the age of fifty-six, at Hamadan, where the following epitaph adorns his tomb : ' The great philosopher, the great physician, Ibn Sina, is dead. His books on philosophy have not taught him the art of living well, nor his books on medicine the art of living long.'

A brief notice must be given of the celebrated physician and philosopher, Ali bin Ridhwan, who died A.D. 1067. He was such a prodigy of precocious learning that he began to lecture on medicine and philosophy at Cairo from his fourteenth year. He afterwards also taught astronomy. At the age of thirty-two he had attained a great reputation as a physician, and was a rich man at sixty. He left more than one hundred books which he had composed, and he himself says : ' I made abridgments of the chief philosophical works of the ancients, and left in this manner five books on philology ; ten on law ; the medical works of Hippocrates and Galen ; the book of plants of Dioskorides ; the books of Rufus, Paulus, Hawi, and Razi ; four books on agriculture and drugs ; four books for instruction in the ' Almagest ' of Ptolemy, and an introduction to the study of it, and to the square of Ptolemy ; as also to the works of Plato, Alexander, Themistios, and Al-Farabi. I purchased all these books, no matter what they cost, and preserved them in chests, although it would have been more profitable to have sold them again rather than have kept them.' Ibn Batlan, a clever physician, was a contemporary of Ibn Ridhwan, and travelled from Baghdad to Egypt only for the purpose of making his acquaintance, but the result does not appear to have been satisfactory to either party. He died A.D. 1063, leaving a number of works on medical and other subjects.

Abu Hamid al-Ghazali was born A.D. 1058. He was considered chiefly as a lawyer and a mystic, but here he will be noticed chiefly as a philosopher and the author of 'The Ruin of Philosophers,' noticed at length by Haji Khalfa in his 'Encyclopaedical Dictionary,' under No. 3764. But Ghazali's most celebrated work is 'The Resuscitation of Religious Sciences,' which is so permeated by the genius of Islam that, according to the general opinion of scholars, the Muhammadan religion, if it were to perish, might again be restored from this work alone. Orthodox fanatics, nevertheless, attacked his works as being schismatic, and they were even burnt in the Mugrib. He was born at Tus (the modern Mashad), in Khurasan, and passed his life partly there, also at Naisapur, Baghdad, Damascus, Egypt, and finally returned to Tus, where he died A.D. 1111. His works are very numerous, and all of them are instructive.

Ibn Bajah (known to Europeans under the name of Avempace) was a philosoper and a poet of considerable celebrity, and a native of Saragossa, in

Spain. He was attacked by some people for his religious opinions, and represented as an infidel and an atheist, professing the doctrines held by the ancient sages and philosophers. Ibn Khallikan defends Ibn Bajah, and says that these statements were much exaggerated, but adds: 'God, however, knows best what his principles were.' Abul Hassan Ali al-Imam, of Granada, was of opinion that Ibn Bajah was the greatest Arab philosopher after Al-Farabi, and places him higher than Ibn Sina and Al-Ghazali. He left numerous logical, grammatical and political works, and died at Fez in A.D. 1138.

Averroes, whose full and correct name is Abul Walid Muhammad bin Rashid, was a celebrated Arab scholar, born at Cordova A.D. 1126, and the author of many writings. He taught in his native town philosophy and medicine, two sciences which appeared for a long time to be inseparable, and the vulgar considered those professing them to be of almost supernatural attainments. The period of Averroes is that of the decadence of Arab dominion in Spain, a period when this great nation also lost the taste for sciences which it had brought to Europe. Considering the prodigious number of works composed by Averroes, who filled at the same time the offices of Imam and Kadi, his entire life must have been one of labour and meditation. He is the author of an Arabic version of Aristotle, but it is not the first which existed in that language, as some of his biographers assert, because this work had been produced already at Baghdad during the brilliant Khalifate of Mamun. There are various manuscripts of Averroes extant treating on physics, pure mathematics, astronomy and astrology, from which it would appear that, in spite of their encyclopædic attainments, the celebrated men of these times still believed in some popular errors. Science was at that time surrounded by a kind of superstitious halo of respect, to which Averroes, like so many others, is indebted for a good part of his renown. He died A.D. 1198, in the city of Morocco; his corpse was transferred to Cordova and there interred.

Medical science had already, under the second Khalif of the house of Abbas (A.D. 754-775), enjoyed the highest honours, which it ever afterwards retained. Great physicians were brought from the Persian hospital of Jondshapur, and between the years A.D. 750 and 850 the number of physicians was considerable, but only the most celebrated will be noticed.

Georgios (Jorjis) bin Bakhtyeshun, of Jondshapur, lived at the commencement of the Abbaside dynasty, and was the author of the book of Pandects. When Al-Mansur was building the city of Baghdad he suffered from pains in his stomach and from impotency, and Georgios, the director of the medical college at Jondshapur, was recommended to him as the most skilled physician of the time.

Accordingly, the Khalif directed Georgios and two of his pupils, Ibrahim and Serjis, to come to Baghdad, appointing Gabriel (Jebrayl), the son of Georgios, as director of the hospital in the place of his father. Georgios cured Al-Mansur, and received from him three thousand ducats for his reward, along with a beautiful slave girl; the latter was, however, returned to the Khalif with thanks, and the remark that, 'being a Christian, he could not keep more than one wife.' From that moment the physician attained free access to the harem, and enjoyed high favour with the Khalif, who greatly pressed him in A.D. 770 to make a profession of Islam; but this he refused to do, and died shortly afterwards, in A.D. 771. Before his death Georgios asked to be allowed to return to Jondshapur, to be buried there with his ancestors. Al-Mansur said, 'Fear God, and I guarantee you paradise.' Georgios replied, 'I am satisfied to be with my ancestors, be it in paradise or be it in hell.' The Khalif laughed, allowed him to return home, and presented him with ten thousand pieces of gold for his travelling expenses.

Gabriel (Jebrayl), the son of the above-named Georgios (Jorjis), was also a celebrated physician. He enjoyed great favour with Harun-ar-Rashid, who used to declare that he would not refuse him anything. When, however, this Khalif fell ill at Tus, and asked Gabriel for his opinion, the latter replied that if Harun had followed his advice to be moderate in sexual pleasure, he would not have been attacked by the disease. For this reply he was thrown into prison, and his life was saved only by the chamberlain Rabi'i, who was very fond of him. Amin, the son and successor of Rashid, followed the advice of Gabriel more than his father did, and would not eat or drink anything without his doctor's sanction. In A.D. 817 Gabriel cured Sehl bin Hasan, who recommended him to Mamun; but Michael, the son-in-law of Gabriel, was his body physician. In A.D. 825 Mamun fell sick, and, as all the medicines of Michael were of no use, Isa, the brother of Mamun, advised him to get himself treated by Gabriel, who had known him from boyhood; but Abu Ishak, the other brother of Mamun, called in Yahya bin Maseweih, and when he could do nothing, then Mamun sent for Gabriel, who restored him to health in three days, and was handsomely rewarded in consequence. When Mamun marched, in A.D. 828, against the Byzantines, Gabriel fell sick and died, whereon the Khalif took Gabriel's son with him on the campaign, he being also an intelligent and skilled physician.

The works of Gabriel are:

(1) A treatise on food and drink, dedicated to Mamun.

(2) An introduction to logic.

(3) Extracts from medical Pandects.

(4) A book on fumigatories.

Isa bin Musa, who flourished about A.D. 833, was also one of the most distinguished physicians of the period. He left the following works:

(1) Book on the forces of alimentary substances.

(2) A treatise for a person who has no access to a physician.

(3) Questions concerning derivations and races.

(4) Book of dreams, indicating why medicines should not be given to pregnant women.

(5) Book of the remedies mentioned by Hippocrates in his treatise on bleeding and cupping.

(6) Dissertation on the use of baths.

Without giving any details about Maseweih, Yahya bin Maseweih, Honein bin Ishak, and Kosta bin Luka, all of whom were distinguished for medical knowledge, some fuller mention must be made of Abu Bakr Ar-Razi (Rhases), who has been described as 'the ablest physician of that age and the most distinguished; a perfect master of the art of medicine, skilled in its practice, and thoroughly grounded in its principles and rules.' He composed a number of useful works on medicine, and some of his sayings have been handed down to us, and are still worthy of record, such as:

(1) When you can cure by a regimen, avoid having recourse to medicine.

(2) When you can effect a cure with a simple medicine, avoid employing a compound one.

(3) With a learned physician and an obedient patient sickness soon disappears.

(4) Treat an incipient malady with remedies which will not prostrate the strength.

Till the end of his life he continued at the head of his profession, finally lost his sight, and died in A.D. 923. A new and much improved edition of Razi's 'Treatise on the Small-Pox and Measles' was published in London in A.D. 1848 by Dr. Greenhill, and an article on him will also be found in Wüstenfeld's 'History of the Arabian Physicians.'

Poetry flourished to a very great extent during the reigns of the early Abbaside Khalifs, and, as all Arab *littérateurs* were more or less poets and writers of verses, it is somewhat difficult to select the most celebrated.

The first collection of Arabic poems was compiled by Al-Mofadhdhal in the work called after him—'Mofadhdhaliat.' He was followed by Abu Amr as Shaibani, by Abu Zaid bin A'us, Ibn-as Sikkit, Muhammad bin Habib, Abu Hatim es Sejastani, and Abu Othman al Mazini. Abu Tammam and Al-Bohtori, the collectors of the two Hamasas, are considered to be the two greatest poets of the third century of the Hijrah (A.D. 816-913). And it may here be observed that in the great bibliographical dictionary of Haji Khalfa, who enumerates seven Hamasas, the names of Ibn-ul Marzaban and of Ibn Demash, each of whom composed one, are not mentioned.

Zukkari made himself a reputation by editing

several of the Mua'llakat, as also the poems of the great pre-Islamite bards, Al-Aasha and Al-Kama, whilst Abu Bakr as Sauli likewise acquired great merit by publishing ten of the master-works of Arabic poetry.

From the many poets of this period some of the most celebrated have been selected—viz., Farazdak, Jarir, Al-Akhtal, Abul-Atahya, Bashshar bin Burd, Abu Nuwas, Abu Tammam, Al-Otbi, Al-Bohtori, Al-Mutanabbi, and An-Nami, and a few biographical details about them will be given, as also some remarks about Al-Mofadhdhal, the first collector and compiler of Arab poetry, and of Abul Faraj-al-Ispahani, the collector of the great anthology called 'Kitab-ul-Aghani,' or the Book of Songs.

Jarir and Al-Farazdak were two very celebrated poets, who lived at the same time and died in the same year, A.D. 728-729. Ibn Khallikan has given their lives at considerable length, and says that 'Jarir was in the habit of making satires on Al-Farazdak, who retorted in the same manner, and they composed parodies on each other's poems.' Jarir always used to say that the same demon inspired them both, and consequently each knew what the other would say. On all occasions they seem to have been excessively rude in verse to each other, and did not at all mind about having recourse to actual insult. The lives of Al-Akhtal, Al-Farazdak, and Jarir, translated from the 'Kitab-ul-Aghani' and other sources, have been given by Mr. Caussin de Perceval in the *Journal Asiatique* for the year 1834. From this it would appear that the verses of these three poets were much discussed during their lifetime, and often compared with the productions of the other poets who followed them. Some writers are in favour of one and some of the other, but the general opinion of them is that their effusions resembled the Arab poetry written before the period of Muhammad much more than any poetry that was written during the reign of the Abbasides. Al-Akhtal belonged to a Christian tribe of Arabs, and was much patronized by the Omaiyide Khalif Abdul Malik (A.D. 684-705), in whose glory and honour he composed many verses, and, indeed, such good ones, that Harun-ar-Rashid used to say no poet had ever said so much in praise of the Abbasides as he (Akhtal) had written in praise of the Omaiyides. He died at an advanced age some years before Jarir and Farazdak, who were much younger men, but the exact year of his death does not appear to have been recorded.

The blind Bashshar bin Burd and Abul-Atahya were two of the principal poets who flourished in the first ages of Islamism, and ranked in the highest class among the versifiers of that period. The former was put to death, or rather beaten, by the orders of the Khalif Al-Mahdi, for certain satirical verses which the poet is said to have written, and from the effects of these strokes of a whip he died in A.D. 783. Abul-Atahya wrote many verses on ascetic subjects, and all his amatory pieces were composed in honour and praise of Otba, a female slave belonging to the Khalif Al-Mahdi, and to whom he appears to have been devotedly attached. He was born A.D. 747, and died A.D. 826.

Abu Nuwas was a poet of great celebrity. His father, Hani, was a soldier in the army of Marwan II., the last Omaiyide Khalif, and the poet was born in A.D. 762, some say in Damascus, others at Busra, and others at Al-Ahwaz. His mother apprenticed him to a grocer, and the boy became acquainted with the poet Abu Osâma, who discovered his talent, and induced him to accompany him to Baghdad. There Abu Nuwas afterwards became celebrated as one of the chief bards at the court of the Khalif, and his most famous Kasida is that which he composed in praise of Amin, the son of Harun-ar-Rashid. According to the critics of his time, he was the greatest poet in Islam, as Amriolkais had been before that period. When Merzeban was asked which he considered the greater poet, Abu Nuwas or Rakâshi, he replied, ' A curse of Abu Nuwas in hell contains more poetry than a laudation of Rakâshi's in paradise.' He was a favourite of Amin, whom his brother Mamun reproached for associating with him, because Abu Nuwas enjoyed the reputation of being the greatest libertine of all the poets.

Sulaiman, the son of Al-Mansur, complained to the Khalif Amin that Abu Nuwas had insulted him with lampoons, and desired him to be punished with death; but Amin replied: 'Dear uncle, how can I order a man to be killed who has praised me in such beautiful verses?' and thereupon recited them.

Mamun, the son of Harun, states that he asked the great critic Yakut bin Sikkit to what poet he gave the preference. He replied: 'Among the pre-Islamite ones to Amriolkais and Al-Aasha, among the older Muslim poets to Jarir and Farazdak, and among the more recent to Abu Nuwas.'

Otbi, having been asked who was the greatest poet, replied: 'According to the opinion of the people, Amriolkais, but according to mine, Abu Nuwas.'

Al-Khasib, the chief of the revenue office in Egypt, once asked Abu Nuwas from what family he came. 'My talents,' replied he, 'stand me instead of noble birth,' and no further questions were asked him. He was a freethinker, who joked about the precepts of Islam. Once a Sunni and a Rafidhi desired him to be the umpire in their quarrel, as to who occupied the most exalted position after the Prophet. He said: 'A certain Yazid,' and on their asking who this Yazid might be, he replied: 'An excellent fellow, who presents me with a thousand dirhems every year.' He used to say that the wine of this world is better than that of the next; and, being asked for the reason, replied: 'This is a sample of the wine of paradise, and for a sample the best is always taken.'

Ismail bin Nubakht said: 'I never saw a man of more extensive learning than Abu Nuwas, nor one who, with a memory so richly furnished, possessed so few books. After his decease we searched his house, and could only find one book-cover containing a quire of paper, in which was a collection of rare expressions and grammatical observations.'

He died on the same day as the mystic Al-Kerkhi, whose corpse was accompanied to the grave by more than three hundred persons, but that of Abu Nuwas by not one. When, however, one of the three hundred exclaimed: 'Was not Abu Nuwas a Muslim? And why do none of the Muslims recite the funeral prayer over his body?' all the three hundred who had assisted at the interment of Kerkhi recited the prayer also over the corpse of Abu Nuwas.

He is considered to have been an equally good narrator, scholar, and poet; and, being asked by Sulaiman bin Sehl what species of poetry he thought to be the best, replied: 'There are no poems on wine equal to my own, and to my amatory compositions all others must yield.' He used to boast that he knew by heart the poems of sixty poetesses, and among them those of Khansa and Leila, as also seven hundred Arjuzat, or poems in unshackled metre, by men. He said that he could compose nothing except when he was in a good humour, and in a shady garden. He often began a Kasida, put it away for several days, and then took it up again to rescind much of it.

According to Abu Amr, the three greatest poets in the description of wine are Aasha, Akhtal, and Abu Nuwas. Abu Hatim al Mekki often said that the deep meanings of thoughts were concealed underground until Abu Nuwas dug them out.

His end was tragic. Zonbor, the secretary, and Abu Nuwas were in the habit of composing lampoons against each other; whereon the former conceived the idea of propagating a satire against Ali, the son-in-law of the Prophet, in the name of Abu Nuwas; and this became the cause of his death. In an already half-drunken circle Zonbor recited the satire on Ali as the work of Abu Nuwas; on which all fell upon the poet, ripped open his belly, and pulled his entrails about till he expired. Others assert that Ismail bin Abu Sehl administered a poisonous potion to Abu Nuwas, because he had composed a lampoon against him; but its operation was so slow that he died only four months after he had drunk it. His death took place at Baghdad in A.D. 810.

Al Otbi was a poet of great celebrity, and taught traditions to the people of Baghdad; but was more generally noted for drinking wine and composing love verses about his beloved Otba. Being of the tribe of Koraish, and of the family of Omaya, he and his father held a high rank, and were regarded as accomplished scholars and elegant speakers. Otbi both composed and collected poems. One of his verses has now acquired the force of a proverb: ' When Sulaima saw me turn my eyes away—and I turn my glances away from all who resemble her—she said: " I once saw thee mad with love ;" and I replied : " Youth is a madness of which old age is the cure." ' He died in A.D. 842.

Abu Tammam Habib, the celebrated poet, according to Ibn Khallikan, 'surpassed all his contemporaries in the purity of his style, the merit of his poetry, and his excellent manner of treating a subject. He is the author of a Hamasa, a compilation which is a standing proof of his great talents, solid information, and good taste in making a selection.' He wrote several other works connected with poets and poetry, composed many Kasidas, and knew by heart, it is said, fourteen thousand verses of that class of compositions called Rajaz, or free metre. The poetry of Abu Tammam was put in order for the first time by Abu Bakr as Sauli, who arranged it alphabetically, according to the rhymes, and then Abul Faraj Ali bin Husain Al-Ispahani classed it according to the subjects. He died at Mosul A.D. 845, about forty years of age, and was buried there; but his verses have survived, and rendered him one of the immortals.

The mantle of the poet Abu Tammam appears to have fallen on Abu Abada Al-Bohtori, who was born in A.D. 821, and, like his predecessor, is also the author of a Hamasa. He appears to have received his first encouragement to persevere as a poet from Abu Tammam, and later on he says: 'I recited to Abu Tammam a poem which I had composed in honour of one of the Humaid family, and by which I gained a large sum of money. When I finished he exclaimed: "Very good! You shall be the prince of poets when I am no more." These words gave me more pleasure than all the wealth which I had collected.' On being asked whether he or Abu Tammam was the better poet, Al-Bohtori replied: 'His best pieces surpass the best of mine, and my worst are better than the worst of his.' Abul-Ala al Maarri, a great philologist and poet (born in A.D. 973, died A.D. 1057), was asked which was the best poet of the three, Abu Tammam, Al-Bohtori, or Al-Mutanabbi; he replied that two of them were moralists, and that Bohtori was the poet. He died A.D. 897. His poems were not arranged in order till Abu Bakr as Sauli collected them and classed them alphabetically by their rhymes, while Abul Faraj Ali bin Husain Al-Ispahani collected them also, and arranged them according to their subjects. A copy of his 'Diwan' is in the Bibliothèque Nationale in Paris.

Al Mutanabbi, or the pretended prophet, a *rôle* to which he aspired, but in which he did not succeed, comes next to the two great poets—Abu Tammam and Al-Bohtori—though some critics consider him to be superior to them. He is, however, generally acknowledged to be a great lyric poet, while many of his best Kasidas refer to the exploits of Saif ad Dawlah, a prince of the Benou Hamdan dynasty in Syria. After leaving him he went to Egypt, then to Persia, Baghdad, and finally Kufa, his native place, near which he was killed in a fight in A.D. 965. It is stated that in this contest Mutanabbi, seeing himself vanquished, was taking to flight, when his slave said to him, 'Let it never be said that you fled from a fight, you who are the author of this verse : " The horse, and the night, and the desert know me (well); the sword also, and the lance, and paper and the pen."'

Upon this he turned back and fought till he was slain, along with his son and his slave. His 'Diwan,' or collection of poems, is well known, and much read in our times, even in India. It has been translated into German.

An-Nami was one of the ablest and most talented poets of his time, but inferior to Mutanabbi, with whom he had some encounters and contests in reciting extemporary verses when they were at the court of Saif ad Dawlah together. He died A.D. 1008 at Aleppo, aged ninety.

Abul-Abbas Al-Mofadhdhal, the collector of the celebrated selection of Arabic poems called the 'Mofadhdhaliat,' which served as a model for the Hamasas, was the first editor of the seven suspended poems, the Mua'llakat, and also one of the earliest of the Arab philologists. He was a native of Kufa, and adhered to the faction of Ibrahim bin Abdallah, who rebelled in A.D. 761 against Al-Mansur, the second Abbaside Khalif. Al-Mansur, however, pardoned Al-Mofadhdhal, and attached him to the household of his son, Al-Madhi, by whose orders Mofadhdhal made a collection of the most celebrated longer poems of the Arabs, one hundred and twenty-eight in number, under the title of the Mofadhdhaliat. This, the oldest anthology of Arabian poets, was first commented upon by his disciple, Al-Aarabi; then two hundred years later by the two great philologists and anthologists, Al-Anbari and An-Nahas; by Merzuk; and lastly by Tibrizi, who is sufficiently known in Europe as the editor and commentator of the Hamasa, published by Freytag with a Latin translation. Mofadhdhal supported himself as a copyist of the Koran, and spent the last portion of his life in mosques doing penance for the satires which he had composed against various individuals. His other works were a book of proverbs, a treatise on prosody, another on the ideas usually expressed in poetry, and a vocabulary. He was held to be of the first authority as a philologist, a genealogist, and a relator of the poems and battle-lays of the desert Arabs. He died A.D. 784.

Abul Faraj Ali bin Husain Al-Ispahani is the collector of the great anthology called 'Kitab-ul-Aghani' (the Book of Songs). This work, which surpasses all former ones of this name, he produced after a labour of forty years, and presented it to Saif ad Dawlah, who gave him a thousand pieces of gold for it, but excused himself at the same time for the smallness of this honorarium. In spite of his other works, and the long string of names given him by Ibn Khallikan, he is best known as Al-Ispahani, and as the author of the Aghani. His family inhabited Ispahan, but he passed his early youth in Baghdad, and became the most distinguished scholar and most eminent author of that city. He was born A.D. 897, and died A.D. 967, in which year also died the great scholar Kali, and the three greatest of his patrons, namely, Saif ad Dawlah, the sovereign of the Benou Hamdan in Syria; Moiz ud Dawlah, the sovereign of the Benou Bujeh in Irak; and Kafur, who governed Egypt in the name of the Akhsid dynasty. The 'Book of Songs,' notwithstanding its title, is an important biographical dictionary, treating of grammar, history and science, as well as of poetry.

Mention can here be made of Abu Muhammad Kassim Al-Hariri, who was one of the ablest writers of his time, and the author of the 'Makâmat Hariri,' a work consisting of fifty oratorical, poetical, moral, encomiastic and satirical discourses, supposed to have been spoken or read in public assemblies. Poets, historians, grammarians and lexicographers look upon the 'Makâmat' (Assemblies or Séances) as the highest authority, and next to the Koran, as far at least as language is concerned. It contains a large portion of the language spoken by the Arabs of the desert, such as its idioms, its proverbs, and its subtle delicacies of expression ; and, according to Ibn Khallikan, any person who acquires a sufficient acquaintance with this book to understand it rightly, will be led to acknowledge the eminent merit of the author, his extensive information, and his vast abilities. A great number of persons have commented on the 'Makâmat,' some in long and others in short treatises, and many consider it to be the most elegantly written, and the most amusing, work in the Arabic language. Hariri was born A.D. 1054, and died at Busra A.D. 1122. He left some other good works in the shape of treatises, epistles, and a great number of poetical pieces, besides those contained in his 'Makâmat.'

There are two translations of the 'Makâmat' into English. One by the Reverend Theodore Preston, printed under the patronage of the Oriental Translation Fund, London, 1850. It contains only twenty of the fifty pieces in verse, with copious notes, while an epitome of the remaining thirty pieces is given at the end of the book. The other by the late Mr. Chenery, which ends with the twenty-sixth assembly or séance. The whole work was edited in Arabic, with a select commentary upon it in French, by Baron Silvestre de Sacy, and this was reprinted in 1847. Ruckert also made a very free translation of it in German verse, which reached a third edition in 1844, but this differs widely from the contents of the original, though it is said to be more pleasing and attractive to a general reader.

After the Muslim legal sciences had been established upon the fourfold foundations of the Koran, tradition, general consent of communities, and the analogies derived therefrom, then philosophy and mathematics began to flourish by translations made either directly from the Greek or through Syriac and Persian.

In former times, during the reign of Nausherwan, a Persian monarch of great renown (A.D. 530-578), there was some intercourse between Persian and Byzantine philosophers; several books on logic and medicine had been translated from Greek into Persian, and from these Abdullah Ibn Al-Mukaffa made translations into Arabic. The literary career of Ibn Al-Mukaffa, who presumed to vie with the eloquence of the Koran, and was considered to be a freethinker, and eventually slain, falls into the reign of Al-Mansur (A.D. 754-775), the second Khalif. But Ibn Al-Mukaffa rendered such services to Arabian literature, that a short sketch of his life will presently be given.

During the reign of Mansur (A.D. 754-775) Greek works were translated, not yet from the original, but from the Persian. During the Khalifate of his son, Mahdi (A.D. 775-785), Abd-Allah bin Hilal translated the celebrated animal fables of Bidpay from Persian into Arabic, under the title of 'Kalilah wa Dimnah,' and they were afterwards versified by Sehl bin Nubakht. In Persian they are known under several titles, such as 'Kalilah wa Dimnah,' the 'Anwar-i Suheli,' and the 'Ayar Danish,' and in Turkish as the 'Humayan-namah.'

Eight years before the seventh Khalif, Mamun (A.D. 812-833), ascended the throne, many Greek and Syrian manuscripts had been collected in Baghdad. These were all preserved there in the library, which was called 'The House of Wisdom,' until Mamun began to utilize them by means of translations. The Khalif appointed the scholars Al-Hajaj, Ibn Mattar, Ibn ul-Batrik, and Selma, to superintend the work, while the three brothers, Muhammad, Ahmed, and Hasan, sons of the astronomer Shakir, were directed to search for and to buy manuscripts. Mamun also sent the two physicians, Yohanna and Kosta, into the Byzantine dominions to bring manuscripts from thence to Baghdad. A new class of scholars was then formed, in the shape of translators, who were employed in translating works from the Greek, the Syriac, and the Persian languages into Arabic.

The translators from the Persian were Musa and Yusuf, the two sons of Khalid, Hasan bin Sehl, and afterwards, Al-Baladori; from the Sanscrit, Munkah the Indian; from the Nabatæan, Ibn Wahshiyah. Science became hereditary, as it were, in the families of the most celebrated scholars; medical science in the family of Bakhtyeshun; translations from Greek works in that of Honein bin Ishak, the most famous of all translators, and a prolific author besides. Maseweih and his son Yahya, Syriac Christians, were both celebrated as physicians and translators of ancient Greek works into Arabic; while Kosta bin Luka, who died in A.D. 932, was also one of the most fertile translators from Greek into Arabic, and, being born a Greek, he was able to correct the translations of Honein bin Ishak and others.

The number of translators, which amounted to about one hundred, might have been increased if Arab literature had further developed itself by incorporating works from other languages; but, as such was not the case, translators appeared very few and far between after the literature had attained to its highest perfection, at the end of the third century of the Hijrah (A.D. 913).

The celebrated Ibn Al-Mukaffa was one of the earliest and best translators. His full name is Abd-Allah Ibn Al-Mukaffa, but before he made his profession of Islam he bore that of Ruzbeh. He was a native of Har, a town in the province of

Fars, and first served as secretary to Daud bin Hobeirah, and then to Isa bin Ali, the uncle of the two first Khalifs of the house of Abbas. He was an excellent poet, letter-writer, and orator, equally skilled in his mother-tongue, the Persian, as in the Arabic language, from the former of which he left the splendid translations of—

(1) 'The Khodanamah,' a legend.
(2) 'The Amirnamah,' or prince-book.
(3) 'Kalilah wa Dimnah.'
(4) 'Merdak.'
(5) 'Biography of Nausherwan.'
(6) 'The Great Book of Manners.'
(7) 'The Small Book of Manners or Good Habits.'
(8) 'The Book of Epistles.'

So far the 'Fihrist'; what follows is from Ibn Khallikan. Ibn Al-Mukaffa was the secretary and most confidential servant of Isa bin Ali, with whom he dined the day before he made his public profession of Islam. Having sat down, he began to eat and to mutter according to the custom of the Magians. 'How,' said Isa, 'you mutter like the Magians, though resolved to embrace Islamism!' to which Ibn Al-Mukaffa replied that he did not wish to pass a single night without being of some religion. In spite of his conversion, he was always suspected of freethinking, like Muti bin Iyas and Yahya bin Zaad, and one day, when Al-Jahiz, the philologist, made the remark that they were persons the sincerity of whose religious sentiments was doubted, one of the learned, on hearing this, said : 'How is it that Al-Jahiz forgets to count himself?'

When Khalil the prosodist was one day asked his opinion about Ibn Al-Mukaffa, he said, 'His learning is greater than his wit;' and the latter, being asked the same question concerning Khalil, replied, 'His wit is greater than his learning.' Being a favourite with the Khalif, he took great liberties with Sofyan, the Governor of Busra, and insulted the memory of his mother. One day Sulaiman and Isa, the uncles of the Khalif Mansur, desired to obtain a letter of amnesty from him for their brother Abd-Allah, and they instructed Ibn Al-Mukaffa to compose one in the strongest terms, which he did, and added to it the following clause, 'Should the Prince of the Believers ever act treacherously towards his uncle Abd-Allah, then may he be divorced from his wives, may his slaves be free, and may his subjects be solved from obedience!' The Khalif's dignity was shocked, and he ordered the writer of this letter of amnesty to be forthwith executed, and the Governor of Busra, whom Ibn Al-Mukaffa had many times insulted, very gladly undertook the duty. Al-Madaini narrates that when Ibn Al-Mukaffa was brought before Sofyan, the latter asked him whether he remembered the insults he had heaped upon his mother, and added, 'May my mother really deserve those insults if I do not get you executed in a manner hitherto unheard of!' He also recalled Ibn Al-Mukaffa's joke about Sofyan's big nose, because he had one day asked the governor, 'How are you and your nose?' On another occasion, when the governor remarked that he never had reason to repent keeping silence, Ibn Al-Mukaffa replied, 'Dumbness becomes you; then why should you repent of it.' Accordingly Sofyan ordered the members of Ibn Al-Mukaffa's body to be chopped off, one after the other, and thrown into a burning oven, into which, last of all, the trunk of his body was also thrown. There are other accounts of his death, viz., that he was strangled in a bath, or shut up in a privy. One opinion, however, generally prevails, that the execution was not a public one. The date of it is uncertain—A.D. 756, 759, and 760, are all given; but the victim was only thirty-six years of age at the time.

A few remarks may be made about the support given to learning and men of letters by the Omaiyide and Abbaside Khalifs, as also by those of the Spanish or Western Khalifate.

The Omaiyide Khalifs, with their capital at Damascus, were generally patrons of science, poetry, architecture, song, and music. But all these branches of knowledge were at that time merely rudimental; and, of the fourteen sovereigns of the dynasty, only five really deserve the name

of protectors of learning; and of these Abdul
Malik (A.D. 684-705), and his son Walid I.
(A.D. 705-715), were the most distinguished.
During the period of their Khalifate there
were not only male, but also some female poets.
All their poems are mostly short, and confined to
amatory, laudatory, or vituperative compositions,
called forth by the momentary circumstances in
which the authors happened to be placed. These
pieces do not represent either deep thought or
profound wisdom, but they show the feelings of
the people, and their state of civilization at the
time in question.

During this Khalifate were also produced the
earliest germs of stylistics, epistolography and
mysticism, all of which were more fully developed
under the Abbasides. The originator of the first
two was the Katib Abd Al-Hamid, secretary to
the last Omaiyide Khalif, and he is designated in
an old Arabic rhyme as 'the father of all
secretaries.' Epistolary writing, it was said,
began with Abd Al-Hamid, and finished with Ibn
Al-Amid. As regards mysticism, the origin of
its doctrines is sometimes assigned to Oweis Al-
Kareni, the Prophet's companion, who disappeared
mysteriously in A.D. 658. But mysticism and
Sufism were subsequently much developed by
Muhi-uddin Muhammad, surnamed Ibn Al-Arabi,
a most voluminous writer on these subjects. He
was born at Murcia, in Spain, A.D. 1165, and after

studying in that country, went to the East, made the pilgrimage, visited Cairo and other cities, and died at Damascus A.D. 1240. He is the author of many works, but the most remarkable of them are 'Revelations obtained at Mecca' and 'Maxims of Wisdom set as Jewels.' Both Makkari the historian, and Von Hammer Purgstall, in his history of Arabian literature from the earliest times, give a long account of him.

Of the Khalifs of the house of Abbas, the second, third, fifth and seventh, viz., Al-Mansur (A.D. 754-775), Al-Mahdi (A.D. 775-785), Harun-ar-Rashid (A.D. 786-809), and Al-Mamun (A.D. 812-833) were the most distinguished as patrons of art, science and literature. But after the translation of the 'Arabian Nights' into European languages, the name of Harun-ar-Rashid became the best known in Europe as the representative of the most brilliant period of the Eastern Khalifate, and as the great protector of Arabic literature.

Baghdad, the capital of the Abbasides, was founded by their second Khalif, Al-Mansur, in A.D. 760, finished in four years, and raised to a high degree of splendour by Harun-ar-Rashid. Originally it was considered only as a great strategic point, and its garrisons were to keep the surrounding country in subjection. Eventually it became the centre of learning and civilization, and an Arab author wrote of it as follows: 'Baghdad is certainly the capital of the world, and the mine of every excellence. It is the city whose inhabitants have always been the first to unfurl the banners of knowledge, and to raise the standard of science ; indeed, their subtlety in all branches of learning, their gentle manners and amiable disposition, noble bearing, acuteness, wit, penetration and talent are deservedly praised.' Baghdad, at the beginning of the ninth century of the Christian era, was the centre of all that was grand and brilliant in the Muhammadan world. Art and commerce, literature and science, were cultivated to a high degree, and the luxury and extravagance of court life exceeded almost the imagination of temperate European minds.

Everything curious, romantic and wonderful, narrated in the ' Nights ' is connected with Harun-ar-Rashid's name, or supposed to have happened in his reign. Thus, his vizier, Jaafar, the Barmekide, the superintendent of his harem, Mesrur, and his spouse, Zobeida, were first made known to novel-readers, and their importance as historical personages were duly appreciated afterwards, when Erpenius, Pococke, Herbelot, and Reiske elucidated the history of the Khalifate by translating the works of the Arab chroniclers Abul-faraj, Al-Makin, and Abul-feda. Later on still further information was made public about the translations made from Greek and Syriac into Arabic during his reign, as also concerning his position, not only as a lover of tales, but as a promoter of jurisprudence, a patron of the medical and mathematical sciences, and a builder of magnificent and useful edifices. His court was also well attended by poets and singers.

Harun was not, indeed, the first prince who made arrangements for translations from the Greek and the Syriac. In this he had been preceded, as already mentioned, by the Omaiyide prince, Khalid, the alchemist. But during the reign of Harun the business of translation was carried on to a much greater extent than it was under his predecessors, the Khalifs Mansur and Mahdi, during whose time translations were undertaken from Greek into Syriac, from Indian (Sanscrit) into Persian, but not yet into Arabic. The translators were mostly Christians and Jews. Theophilos of Edessa, the Maronite translator of Homer and of other Greek classics into Syriac, was an astronomer and an historian. Both he and the physician Georgios, son of Bakhtyeshun, from the university of Jondshapur, were Christians. Nubakht, the astronomer of the Khalif Mansur, was a Magian (Zoroastrian). Yahya bin Maseweih, Harun's physician, translated medical works. Hajaj bin Yusuf bin Matta dedicated his first edition of the elements of Euclid to Harun, and the second to Mamun.

As the family of the Barmekides played an important part, not only in politics, but also in literature, until its chief members were annihilated by Harun's orders, a brief notice of them may here be given.

Khalid bin Barmek was the son of a priest at the fire temple of Nevbehar in Balkh, and became in course of time vizier of the first Abbaside Khalif, and was retained in that office by the second Khalif, Al-Mansur, and by the third, Al-Mahdi. He died A.D. 780.

Yahya, the son of Khalid, not only himself became the vizier of Harun, but also his two sons, Fadhl and Jaafar. Yahya was very liberal, and gave away sometimes considerable sums of money for very small services, or, indeed, for no service at all. After his son Jaafar had been executed, Yahya was thrown into prison, along with his other son, Fadhl, at Old Rakka, where he died in A.D. 805, at the age of seventy or seventy-four.

Fadhl, the son of Yahya, was more liberal but less eloquent than his brother Jaafar. Harun esteemed the two brothers so highly that he entrusted his son Muhammad to the care of Fadhl, and his son Mamun to the care of Jaafar. Afterwards he made Jaafar his vizier, and sent Fadhl to be Governor of Khurasan. There Fadhl built mosques, reservoirs of water and caravanserais, augmented the army, and attracted numbers of emigrants to the country, whereby he gained the approval of Harun, who ordered his poets to sing his praises. After the execution of Jaafar, Harun took Yahya, with his son Fadhl and all the Barme-

kides, to Rakka, giving Yahya the option to go
where he liked; but he preferred to be imprisoned
with his son in Rakka. There Fadhl died in
A.D. 809, and when Harun was informed of his
death, he said . 'My own is not far,' and died a few
months afterwards in Tus, the modern Mashad.
The death of Fadhl, as a generous patron, was
bewailed by several poets, such as Abul Hojna,
Otbi, Abu Nuwas, and others. Fadhl was also
notable for his filial piety, and when the use of cold
water injured the health of his father whilst they
were in prison, he used to warm the water by
placing a pot of it on his own stomach.

Jaafar (the brother of Fadhl and a son of
Yahya), who was slain A.D. 802, is to be mentioned
here, not for his tragic fate, which is well known,
but rather for his literary attainments, especially
his oratory and his style, in both of which he
excelled. From his long biography, written by
Ibn Khallikan, there will be given here only some
extracts relating to science and literature. He
was a great master of speech, and expressed his
thoughts with much elegance. In one night he
endorsed more than a thousand petitions addressed
to the Khalif with his decisions, all of which were
in perfect concordance with the law. His in-
structor in jurisprudence had been Abu Yusuf the
Hanifite, whom his father Yahya had appointed
to teach him. The favour enjoyed by Jaafar with
Harun-ar-Rashid was so great that this Khalif

caused one robe to be made with two separate collars, which they both wore at the same time. Ibn Khallikan narrates the traditions relating to the fall of Jaafar and his family; the one refers to his amours with Abbasa, the sister of Harun, and to the birth of a child; the other to the escape of a member of Ali's family entrusted to Jaafar's guardianship by Harun. The true cause was probably the Khalif's envy of the power, wealth, and generosity of the Barmekides, along with the backbitings of their enemies. Jaafar was slain at Al-Omr in the district of Al-Anbar, his head and the trunk of his body were set up opposite to each other on the two sides of the bridge of Baghdad, and his death was lamented by various poets.

After Mamun (A.D. 812-833) the most intellectual Khalif appears to have been Radhi-billah (A.D. 934-940). His poems were collected in a Diwan. He was the last Khalif who presided not only over the Government as a sovereign, but also over the pulpit as Imam; indeed, he may be said to be the terminal point of the power, brilliancy and independence of the house of Abbas, which henceforth gradually declined till its final extinction with the conquest of Baghdad by the Mughals in A.D. 1258.

The great chess-player, Abu-bakr as Sauli, bears witness, in Masudi's 'Meadows of Gold,' to the great accomplishments of Radhi-billah, and to his

love of the sciences. Of games, chess and nerd *
flourished during his reign, and although the perfection of song and of lute-playing had already
passed away, singers and musicians are still mentioned. Of the amusements of the court, hunting
appears to have flourished most, and the learned
poet Koshajim, who wrote on the game of nerd,
also left instructive poems on the chase. Radhi-
billah appears to have been fond of books of travel
and of natural history, and of the society of men
of letters and of science, and liked listening to
recitals on the history, politics, and glory of the
old Persian kings.

Of the Spanish Khalifs, mention only will be
made of the ninth sovereign of the Benou Omaiyide
dynasty in Andalusia, viz., Hakim II., who died
A.D. 976. Among the five Arab rulers of Spain—
viz., three Abd-ar-Rahmans and two Hakims—
who have acquired everlasting fame in history as
special friends of science and patrons of learned
men, Abd-ar-Rahman III. and Hakim II. are the
greatest and most prominent. They stand in the

* Nerd.—This game is mentioned as early as the Shah-
Namah, the author of which, Firdausi, was of opinion that it is
of genuine Persian, and not of Indian origin, like chess; but
this assertion is not necessarily correct. Hyde has described
the game in his 'Historia Nerdiludii,' and it resembles somewhat the German puff and triktrak, and the English backgammon. It is played on a board divided into black-and-white
compartments, with a black and a white house in the centre.
The moves are made according to the numbers that come up
on the throw of two dice.

Arab literary history of the West as high as Harun and his son Mamun do in the history of the literature of the East. As Mamun was the greatest of the Benou Abbas Khalifs of Baghdad who promoted science and art, so Hakim II. was the greatest of the Benou Omaiyides in Cordova. From his earliest youth he had received a most careful scientific education, and applied his energies to study, as he could not devote them to public affairs on account of the long duration of his father's reign, from A.D. 912 to 961. Hakim's father, Abd-ar-Rahman III., invited the learned Abu Ali Ismail Al Kali, the philologist and author, from the court of Baghdad, where he enjoyed the greatest consideration with the Khalif Mutwakkil, to Cordova, and entrusted him with the education of his son, who, later on, composed a Diwan (collection of poems), divided into twenty parts, bearing, like the Surahs, or Chapters of the Koran, the most sublime objects of nature as titles, such as 'Heaven,' 'the Stars,' 'the Dawn,' 'the Night,' etc. Hakim pursued his studies under Kali for twenty years, with as much pleasure as advantage, and after ascending the throne, science and art still remained his companions. When his father died, and he assumed the Government, he led the funeral procession, surrounded by his Andalusian, Slavonic, and Mograbin body-guard, and interred the corpse with the greatest pomp in the mausoleum of Rozafa, and after that accepted the homage of his Viziers, Amirs, Kayids, and Kadis. Astrologers and poets heralded at Cordova and in the whole of Andalusia the continuation of the father's prosperous reign by his son, and spoke the truth this time.

Hakim, who had already as a youth been fond of books, now, when he became sovereign, fully satisfied this predilection, which had grown to be a passion. He spared neither trouble nor expense in collecting in his Merwan palace the rarest and most costly books in every branch of science from all countries. He sent special commissioners to Egypt, Syria, Irak, and Persia to purchase books. At Baghdad, Muhammad bin Turkhan was charged with the business of purchasing books, or getting them copied, for which purpose he had an establishment of calligraphers and stenographers; because of some books beautiful, and of others rapidly made, copies were required. He procured all the genealogies, all the histories, and all the poems of the Arabs; all works on law and jurisprudence, on grammar, rhetoric, philosophy, philology, mathematics, astronomy, arithmetic and geography, composed in Arabic. Thus the library of the Merwan palace became not only the richest in Islam, but also the best arranged, by the care which he bestowed on it. The catalogue consisted of forty-four fascicles, each of fifty leaves, so that the whole constituted a volume of two thousand two hundred leaves, two-fifths of which were filled with titles of poetical works only. In this catalogue the titles of the books were inserted, with the names of their authors, their descent, birth-place, the year of their birth and of their decease, in the most accurate manner, to serve as a model for other libraries, of which Spain contained so many. This library alone is said to have consisted of six hundred thousand volumes, a number never surpassed by any earlier or later libraries in Islam.

To his two brothers, who loved the sciences as ardently as himself, Hakim entrusted the care of the libraries, and of public instruction, appointing Abdul Latif to be the chief librarian, and another man to be the director of studies. He kept up intercourse with the great scholars of the East and of the West, with sundry persons in Syria, with learned men in Egypt, and with Abul Faraj Al-Ispahani (author of the great anthology 'Kitab-ul-Aghani') in Irak, giving houses and salaries to those who chose to reside at his court.

A few words must be said about the establishment of places of learning which were celebrated at the time. The first university, in the sense in which such an institution is at present understood, was flourishing in Syria long before any seat of learning of this kind had been established in Europe; and there was another in Egypt. The first institution was called 'The Society of the Brethren of Purity,' and the second (opened at Cairo on the 24th May, A.D. 1005) was founded by Al-Hakim-bramrillah, and bore the name of Dar-ul Hikmat, or Abode of Wisdom. It was under this same name that the library of the Khalifs was formerly known at Baghdad. Later on the great vizier Nizam-ul-Mulk founded a high school at Baghdad, in A.D. 1066. It was not the first that had been established in Islam, but it eclipsed all others of the kind by the abilities of the professors who worked there, viz., the Imam Abu Ishak Shirazi, Al-Ghazali, and others. With the Society of the Brethren of Purity, mentioned above, there were two men closely connected, viz., Al-Tavhidi, who died A.D. 985, and Al-Majridi, who died A.D. 1004, the former in the East, the latter in the West, and both of them are deserving of the general name of philosopher. So much for the Eastern Khalifates. As regards the Western Khalifate, still greater attention was paid to education and learning there. The schools and lectures were attended by many Europeans, who were not, perhaps, sufficiently grateful to the Arabs for keeping up a progress in literature and science while Europe itself was struggling for emancipation from the dark ages which followed the higher cultures of Greece and of Rome.

Third Period.

From the fall of Baghdad, in A.D. 1258, to the present time.

The conquest of Baghdad by the Mughals is a

most remarkable period, not only in the literature, but also in the history, of the Arabs. It marks the final extinction of the Abbaside dynasty, from whom the ancient power and glory had vanished to such a degree that the authority of the Khalifs may almost literally be said to have been confined to the city only. Halaku Khan, the brother of the grand Khan Kubilai, and grandson of Jenghiz Khan, took and sacked Baghdad, keeping the Khalif imprisoned for some time, but slaying him at last, with his sons and several thousand Abbasides. Al-Mustaa'sim was the thirty-seventh and last Khalif of the house of Abbas, which had reigned over five hundred years, and was now extinguished.

Halaku Khan attacked Baghdad by the advice of Khojah Nasir-uddin Tusy, the great Persian astronomer and mathematician. Nasir-uddin had entered the service of the last prince of the Assassins only for the purpose of avenging himself on the Khalif, who had disparaged one of his works. When, however, he became aware of Halaku's power, he not only betrayed his new master to him, but led the Mughal conqueror also to Baghdad. After the burning of the library at Alamut (the stronghold of the Assassins, where they kept their literary treasures) and the sacking of Baghdad by Halaku Khan, the erection of the astronomical observatory at Maragha, under the direction of Nasir-uddin Tusy, was the first sign that Arab civilization and the cultivation of science had not been entirely extinguished by Tartar barbarism. The learned viziers who stood by the side of the conqueror, such as the two brothers Juvaini, were Persians, and therefore hardly belong to the history of Arab literature. But the fact that one of these two historians now wrote 'The Heart Opener,' also implies that the invasion of the barbarians had not quite put an end to literary activity.

More than ten historians flourished at the beginning of this period whose names terminated with 'din,' such as Baha-uddin, Imad-uddin, Kamal-uddin, etc., and they were contemporaries of the Arab Plutarch Ibn Khallikan, already mentioned and described in the preceding period.

The 'Alfiyya,' or Quintessence of Arab Grammar, was written in verse by Jamal-uddin Abu Abd-allah Muhammad, known under the name of Ibn Malik. The author died in A.D. 1273-1274; but his work has lived, and it is looked upon as a good exponent of the system. The Arab text has been published, with a commentary upon it in French, by Silvestre de Sacy, A.D. 1834.

During the eighth century of the Hijrah (A.D. 1301-1398), there lived three distinguished men, one famed as a geographer and traveller, and the other two as historians, viz., Ibn Batuta, Abul Feda, and Ibn Khaldun. The first-named left his native town, Tangiers, in A.D. 1324, and travelled all over the East, performing his pilgrimage to Mecca in A.D. 1332. The travels of Ibn Batuta were translated by the Rev. S. Lee, and published by the Oriental Translation Fund, as their first work, in A.D. 1829. This traveller has been noticed by Kosegarten in a Latin treatise, and his travels have been also translated into French, with the Arabic text above, by C. Defremery and R. Sanguinetti, at the expense of the French Government (1874-1879).

Abul Feda Ismail Hamawi is well known as an historian, and is frequently mentioned by Gibbon as one of his authorities. He wrote an account of the regions beyond the Oxus, and also an abridgment of universal history down to his own time, and as he is supposed to be very exact, and his style elegant, his works are very much esteemed. He died A.D. 1345, having succeeded his brother Ahmad as King of Hamat in Syria, A.D. 1342.

Ibn Khaldun, the African philosopher, was born in Tunis, A.D. 1332, and passed his youth in Egypt. He served a short time as Chief Justice at Damascus, and returned to Egypt, where he became Supreme Judge, and died there A.D. 1406. His principal and most remarkable work is the 'History of the Arabs, the Persians, and the Berbers.'

During the ninth century of the Hijrah (A.D. 1398-1495) Arabian literature can still boast of a few great names. Ibn-Hajar was not only the continuator of Ibn Kesir's universal history, called 'The Beginning and the End,' but also the author of biographies of celebrated men who had lived during the preceding century, and of other works besides. He died A.D. 1449. Ibn Arabshah was the writer of a history of Timour, or Tamerlane, which has some celebrity, and has been translated into Latin and French. He was a native of Damascus, and died there A.D. 1450.

Majr-uddin Muhammad Bin Yakub, surnamed Firuzabadi, a learned Persian, was the author of the largest and most celebrated Arabic dictionary in existence at the time, called the 'Qânûs,' or Ocean, a standard work to this day, and always greatly praised, and also used by European lexicographers.

Taki-uddin, of Fez, composed the best history of Mekka, and A'ini, who died A.D. 1451, wrote two celebrated historical works. But the greatest historian of this time was Al-Makrisi, whose proper name was Taki-uddin Ahmad, and who was born at Makris, near Baalbec, in A.D. 1366. He early devoted himself to the study of history, geography, astrology, etc., at Cairo, and his Egyptian history and topography is still an important work, describing the state of the country and its rulers. He died at Cairo, A.D. 1442. Some of his works have been translated into French and Latin, and are still referred to.

In honour of Sayuti, that colossus of learning,

who cultivated, according to the spirit of his times, so many sciences, and dealt with them practically, this might be called the poly-historical and poly-geographical period. Julal-uddin Sayuti is said to be the author of some four hundred works, and he died in A.D. 1505, some twelve years before the conquest of Egypt by Selim I., the Sultan of Turkey, when independent Arab literature under Arab sovereigns came to an end. It is true enough that not only in Egypt and Syria, but also in Turkey and Persia, Arabic books were written afterwards, but more under foreign protection, although in the two first-named countries Arabic is the language of the people, while in the last two it occupies nearly the same position that Latin does in European universities and in the Roman Catholic Church.

In the tenth century of the Hijrah (A.D. 1495-1592) the generally prevalent belief that the world would, at the completion of it, come to an end, contributed much to the gradual decay of science and literature. The case is somewhat analogous to the superstition in Europe some six hundred years previously, when the Christian era attained its millennium, which was considered to carry with it the same catastrophe. This prophecy, believed to be true, contributed in some measure to slacken authority as well as exertion, and the power of Islamitic countries really sank; but this might have been predicted without any prophetic foresight.

In one part of Islam, the ruin of Muhammadan countries thus prophesied was accomplished twenty-one years before the end of the thousandth year, that is in the 979th year of the Hijrah, A.D. 1571, by the total expulsion of the Moors from Spain. Granada itself had succumbed already, seventy-nine years before, and the unwieldy palace of the kings of Spain (still unfinished) had risen by the side of the lofty arcades of the Alhambra, still a lovely specimen of Moorish artistic design and architecture.

The tenth century of the Hijrah (A.D. 1495-1592), which was the first of the decay of Arab literature, is to be considered as the period when the political importance of Turkey culminated in the reign of Sulaiman the Law-giver. There were, however, four authors of celebrity who wrote both in Arabic and in Turkish. Ibn Kamal Pasha, the surname of Mufti Shams-uddin Ahmad bin-Sulaiman, who died A.D. 1534, wrote on history in Turkish, and on law in Arabic: the Mufti Abu Sa'ud acquired great renown by his numerous Fetwas (legal decisions), approving of the political institutions of Sulaiman ; Ibrahim of Aleppo is the author of the ' Molteka ' (Confluence of Two Seas), which embodies the essence of Muslim law, according to the Hanifi ritual ; and lastly, Birgeli, otherwise known as Mulla Muhammad Ibn Pir Ali ul-Birkali, was equally great as a dogmatist and as a grammarian. He wrote in Arabic ' The Unique Pearl ; or, The Art of Reading the Koran,' and died

A.D. 1573. Special mention, too, must be made of Mulla Ahmad Bin Mustafa, the celebrated Arabian, whom Haji-Khalfa always calls by the more euphonious name of Abul-Khair (Father of Wisdom). This author is worthy of notice, on account of the Arabic works he wrote on biographical, historical, and especially encyclopædic subjects. His 'Key of Felicity' will remain for ever the best encyclopædia of Arabian sciences, representing as it does their division among the Arabs, with notices of the works of scholars in every branch of them in a most compact and comprehensive manner. He died A.D. 1560.

The three most celebrated calligraphers of this century were Hamdallah, who died A.D. 1518; Mir Ali, who died A.D. 1544; and Muhammad Hussain Tabrizi, who died A.D. 1574. Their names are just as celebrated for Thuluth and Talik writing as were formerly those of Ibn Bawwab, of Ibn Hilal, and of Yakut are for Naskhi. In Egypt and Syria the characters used were always more beautiful than those of Andalusia, which survived in the Mugrib (North of Africa).

Here, perhaps, it may be stated that the art of Arabic writing came into existence but a very short time before Muhammad. 'It was Abu Ali bin Mukla who first took the present system of written characters from the style of writing employed by the people of Kufa, and brought it out under its actual form. He had, therefore, the merit of

8

priority, and it may be added that his handwriting was very elegant. But to Ibn Al Bawwab pertains the honour of rendering the character more regular and simple, and of clothing it in grace and beauty.' In other words, Ibn Mukla was the first who changed the Kufic into the new Naskhi character, which Ibn Bawwab improved after him by imparting rotundity and clearness to the new letters, and which Ibn Yakut Al-Mausili brought afterwards to the greatest perfection in A.D. 1200.

Ibn Mukla, who was born in A.D. 885, and died A.D. 941, was vizier to the Khalifs Al-Kahir-billah and Al-Radhi-billah ; but, falling into disfavour through the intrigues of his enemies, he first had his hand cut off in A.D. 937, and eventually his tongue was torn out, and he was allowed to perish in the dungeon without any assistance being offered to him.

Ibn-al-Bawwab, the Penman, is said to have possessed a skill in penmanship to which no other person ever attained in ancient or modern times. He died at Baghdad A.D. 1032, and the following verses were composed as his elegy :

> 'Thy loss was felt by the writers of former times,
> And each successive day justifies their grief.
> The ink-bottles are therefore black with sorrow,
> And the pens are rent through affliction.'

During the eleventh century of the Hijrah (A.D. 1592-1689) there lived Mustafa bin Abdullah Katib Jelaby, otherwise known as Haji Khalfa, and commonly called Mustafa Haji Khalfa, a man of science as a Turkish historian and geographer, but an Arabic encyclopædist and bibliographer. He was the compiler of a work containing many thousands of titles of Arab, Persian, and Turkish books, with the names of their authors. Fluegel edited this great work under the title of 'Lexicon Enciclopædicum et Bibliographicum,' with a Latin translation in seven bulky volumes, and it is an extremely valuable work of reference, put together with the most astonishing and persevering care, and consulted by all who desire information on Arabic, Persian, and Turkish literature. This was printed by the Oriental Translation Fund between A.D. 1835 and 1850, and will always remain as one of the most valuable works printed by that most useful society, whose extinction must ever be regretted by all Orientalists and persons interested in Oriental literature. Haji Khalfa wrote another interesting work, giving a detailed account of the maritime wars of the Turks in the Mediterranean and Black Sea and on the Danube, which has been translated by Mr. James Mitchell. The date of Haji Khalfa's death is uncertain. He is known to have been alive in A.D. 1622, and still in 1652, and he is supposed to have died in A.D. 1657.

The works of Abul Khair, previously mentioned, and of Haji Khalfa, embody a mass of information, and constitute the top of the pyramid of encyclopædical and biographical works, after which nothing worthy of mention has been written on these subjects. The basis of this pyramid had been already laid by An-Nadim, the author of the 'Fihrist,' who flourished A.D. 987, and by Ibn Khallikan, who died A.D. 1282.

During this century (A.D. 1592-1689) of the most sanguinary wars, revolutions and dethronements, the condition of Arab literature in the Ottoman Empire was neither progressive nor satisfactory. Nevertheless, the study of the sciences, and especially the linguistic and juridical branches of them, were fostered not only in Constantinople, but also in Syria and Egypt, in consequence of the institution of the body of Ulema, established by Muhammad II., the Conqueror (A.D. 1451-1481), and improved by Sulaiman I., the Lawgiver (A.D. 1520-1566), which sheltered the cultivation of science from the storms of war within the inviolable precincts of religion.

Mention may be made of Muhammad-Al-Amin, the learned philologist and lawyer of Damascus, who was born in that town about the middle of the eleventh and died the beginning of the twelfth century of the Hijrah, and produced a dozen respectable works, the principal of which bears the title of 'The Biographies of the Celebrated Men of the Eleventh Century,' A.H. He gives an account of a couple of hundred scholars, who represented in Egypt and in Syria the last rays of the setting sun of Arabian literature.

Next to Muhammad-Al-Amin another author of about a dozen works is to be noticed, namely, Ahmad-Al-Makkari, whose principal work was a history of the Muhammadan dynasties in Spain, which was translated from the copies in the library of the British Museum, and illustrated with critical notes on Spanish history, geography and antiquities, by Pascual de Gayangos, and printed for the Oriental Translation Fund of Great Britain and Ireland in A.D. 1840-43. Makkari also wrote a history of Fez and Morocco, as well as an account of Damascus. He died at Cairo A.D. 1631.

Besides some historians, grammarians, philologists and poets, the eleventh century of the Hijrah (A.D. 1592-1689) produced in Syria and Egypt even astronomers and physicians, who distinguished themselves as scholars. Of writers of light literature Khafaji may be named as the chief. He composed a Diwan of ardent love poems, with two anthologies, containing specimens of verses from a couple of poets, his contemporaries. He died A.D. 1658. A few more writers might be mentioned; but their efforts strongly mark the decline of Arabic literature in the East, the cultivation of which, however, was henceforth more energetically pursued in Europe, where many works have been printed and translated.

With the twelfth century of the Hijrah (A.D. 1689-1786) the history of original Arab literature may be said to have terminated, and its genius to have disappeared. A revival, however, of Arabian learning is taking place in Egypt, Syria, and North Africa, but in accordance with European models, and chiefly under European auspices. All original research has long been extinct, even among those populations whose vernacular is the Arabic language; and consequently it is the former, and not the present state of Arab literature, which is the most interesting to the people of to-day.

The presses of Constantinople, Cairo, Algiers, Beyruth, and some other places, reproduce old Arabic works of value, but more translations from European languages than original compositions are printed and lithographed. From Bombay, where more than fifty presses are at work, large quantities of books are exported to countries beyond the British possessions. These books treat generally of religion, poetry, history, or medicine; but as they deal more with ancient than with modern knowledge, they do not tend to propagate progress.

But though Arab literature has decayed, the faith of Islam is still active and energetic. It is estimated that one hundred and eighty millions of human beings still follow the precepts of the Prophet, and daily turn their faces to Mecca, which for them has been, and still is, the cradle of their faith, the touchstone of their religion, and the idol of their hearts.

CHAPTER III.

ABOUT MUHAMMAD.

A MANUAL of Arabian history and literature would hardly be complete unless some special mention of Muhammad was introduced. As previously stated, his Koran forms the basis of the literary edifice of Arab literature, while he himself undoubtedly holds the first place in Arab history. As the author and founder of a new religion, which both during his lifetime and after his death was accepted with a marvellous rapidity, and is still being accepted in various parts of Africa, it must be admitted that he was an extraordinary person. At the beginning of what may be called his inspired life at Mecca, he stood forth as a reformer, preacher, and apostle. But, though full of enthusiasm and belief in the great cause that he advocated, he was, without doubt, from the commencement to the end of his career, a practical man of business, which Buddha and Jesus certainly were not.

The life of Muhammad has been written in

many languages, and with such voluminous details, that it is hardly necessary to enter into these details very minutely here. Sir William Muir's works on the subject are graphic, descriptive, and full of interesting matter, while a lengthy article on the subject of Muhammad and Muhammadism, in the third volume of the 'Dictionary of Christian Biography,' from the pen of the late Rev. G. P. Badger, is one of extraordinary interest. A perusal of the above-named works, with Hughes's 'Dictionary of Islam' as a reference book, will give the ordinary English reader as much information as is likely to be required in the ordinary course of things.

But by way of preface to certain remarks upon Muhammad as a reformer, preacher, and apostle at Mecca, as pope and king at Madinah, as author of the Koran, founder of a religion, legislator, military leader, and organizer of the Arabs into a nation, it is perhaps necessary to give a rapid summary of the principal events of a life which has had such an influence upon so many people, and which has filled so many pages. This summary will be as brief as possible:

His birth, August, A.D. 570, at Mecca, his father having died some months previously.

His christening by the name of Muhammad, i.e., the Praised One. His grandfather Abdul-Muttalib, who gave him the name, said it was given to him 'in the hope that his grandson would be praised by God in heaven, and by God's creatures on earth.'

His bringing up in the desert of the Benou-Saad by a Badawin nurse, one Halimah, the wife of Harith, for five years.

His mother Aminah took him, aged six, to Madinah to present him to his maternal relations there. She died on the return journey, A.D. 576.

Under the guardianship of his grandfather Abdul Muttalib (who loved him dearly) for two years, from six to eight, when Abdul died, A.D. 578.

Under the guardianship of his uncle Abu Thaleb, the uterine brother of his father, Abd-Allah.

When about twelve years old, Muhammad accompanied his uncle, Abu Thaleb, into Syria on a mercantile expedition. His first visit to that country, and his experiences there, A.D. 582.

His presence, during the sacrilegious war, at a battle between certain tribes at or near Okatz, where he assisted his uncle, who took part in the fight.

His attendance at sundry preachings and poetical and eloquent recitations at Okatz, where it is said he imbibed the first lessons of the art of poetry and the power of rhetoric, and also acquired certain religious sentiments.

His life as a shepherd in the neighbourhood of Mecca, and the ideas that such a lonely life, face to face with nature, would perhaps inspire.

His acquisition of the title of Al-Amin, the Trustworthy.

His second visit to Syria, when twenty-five years old (A.D. 595), on a mercantile expedition, as agent to the widow Khadijah, and his acquisition of religious impressions there.

His successful business, and his marriage on his return to Khadijah, fifteen years his senior in age, A.D. 595.

Six children born to Muhammad by Khadijah, most of whom died young.

The rebuilding of the Kaabah in A.D. 605, in which Muhammad accidentally takes a prominent part.

His solitary contemplations and studies, from the age of twenty-five to forty, at Mecca, and in the cave on Mount Hira near Mecca.

Here it is important to bear in mind the foregoing experiences in the life of Muhammad as we approach the period of his alleged revelations. There can be no doubt that by this time he had acquired, as well through his own observation and inquiry, as through intimate converse with Barakah, reputed the most learned Arab of the age, considerable acquaintance with the dogmas of Judaism and Christianity; that he had some knowledge of the Bible, the Talmud, and the Gospels; that he was thoroughly versed in Arab legendary lore, and that, being gifted with a ready flow of speech, an ardent imagination, together with a bold, enterprising spirit, he was well equipped for carrying out that grand social and religious revolution among his countrymen which he contemplated.

His yearnings after religious truth and his first poetic productions.

His mental depressions.

His first inspirations from the angel Gabriel, A.D. 610.

His account of his visions to his wife, who became the first convert to al-Islam, or the creed of Muhammad.

His next converts were Ali, his adopted son and cousin; Zaid-bin-Harithah, also an adopted son; Warakah; and Abdul-Kaabah-bin-Kuhafah, one of the most influential and learned men of Mecca, on conversion named Abd Allah, and afterwards called Abu Bakr, 'The Father of the Virgin,' 'The Companion of the Cave,' 'The Second of the Two,' 'The True,' 'The Sighing,' etc., and who eventually became the first Khalifah, or Successor.

Other conversions followed; viz., Saad, Zobeir, Talha; Othman bin Affan, the third Khalifah, or Successor, after Abu Bakr and Omar; Abdar-Rahman, and several more.

The injunctions of Muhammad to his converts were then as follows: 'The duty of believing in one God; in a future reward reserved for the righteous in another life, and a future punishment for the wicked; of acknowledging himself as the Apostle of God, and of obeying him as such; of practising ablution ; of offering up prayer according to certain specified rules.' These, he said, did not constitute a new religion, but merely restored the ancient religion of Abraham to its pristine purity. His teachings, he maintained, were revelations conveyed to him by Gabriel, and he simply repeated what the angel communicated to him.

His assumption of the title of Apostle of God, in whose name he now spoke, A.D. 610.

His frequent revelations for three years, and the commencement of his public preaching to the Koraish, who would not listen, but regarded him as a half-witted poet.

His denouncement of idolatry, and the consequent persecutions of himself and his followers by the Koraish.

Conversions in the house of Arcam, afterwards styled the House of Islam.

The first emigration to Abyssinia of some of his followers by his advice, and their speedy return, A.D. 615.

The lapse of Muhammad and his idolatrous concession, but afterwards disowned and disavowed.

The second emigration to Abyssinia, A.D. 615-616.

The conversion of Hamzah and Omar and thirty-nine adherents of the latter — a great event, A.D. 615-616.

The Koraish try to come to terms with Muhammad, but fail.

The prohibition of all intercourse with Muhammad and his followers by order of the Koraish, and a general persecution.

The excommunication of Muhammad and of the descendants of Hisham and Muttalib, which lasted more than three years, A.D. 617-620.

The death of Muhammad's first wife, Khadijah, in December, A.D. 619, and of his uncle, Abu Thaleb, in January, 620.

His critical position. He seeks an asylum at Taif, but not being well received, returns to Mecca, remaining there in comparative retirement.

His marriage, A.D. 620, with Saudah-bint-Zamaah, the widow of one Sukran, and his betrothal to Ayesha, the daughter of Abu Bakr, then only eight years old.

The first meeting at the Pilgrimage of a party from Yathrib (Madinah), to whom Muhammad expounds his doctrines. The listeners profess their belief in him, and propose to advocate his cause in their native place. March, A.D. 620.

The conference at Akabah, a hill on the north side of Mecca, with the men of certain tribes resident at Yathrib, who took an oath to be faithful to Muhammad and his religion. This is called 'the first pledge of Akabah.' April, A.D. 621.

The despatch of Musaab, a Meccan disciple, to Yathrib, for the purpose of giving instruction in the Koran and in the rites of the new religion.

The Night of the Ladder, or the miraculous

journey first from Mecca to Jerusalem upon the beast called al-Burak, and then the ascent from Jerusalem to heaven, under the guidance of Gabriel, and what he saw there. Apparently a dream or vision. A.D. 621.

Second meeting at Akabah, called 'the second pledge of Akabah,' and engagements ratified. March, A.D. 622.

Distrust of the Koraish. Proposal to kill Muhammad, who had advised his followers to flee to Yathrib. April and May, A.D. 622.

In June, A.D. 622, Muhammad himself secretly leaves Mecca with Abu Bakr. They first go to a cave in Mount Thur, about three miles to the south of Mecca, and reach Yathrib (henceforward to be called Al Madinah, 'The City' *par excellence*) a few days afterwards.

On his way there, at Kuba, a village two miles to the south of Madinah, Muhammad laid the foundation of a mosque called 'The Fear of God.' This was the first temple raised by Islam.

Enthusiastic reception at Madinah, a charter drawn up, and Muhammad assumes the reins of both spiritual and temporal sovereignty.

His family arrives from Mecca.

He completes his house and mosque at Madinah, and draws up a bond of union between the Ansars, or auxiliaries, of Madinah and the Al Muhajirun, or emigrants from Mecca, who were the first to embrace Islam.

Marriage with Ayesha consummated, January, A.D. 623.

Marriage of Fatimah, Muhammad's daughter, to Ali bin Abu Thaleb, the adopted son and cousin of Muhammad, June, A.D. 623.

The call to prayer ; the Kiblah, or place to which the face was turned in prayer, changed from Jerusalem to Mecca ; the fast of Ramadhan, and the tithe, or poor rate, instituted. Friday appointed as the day for public service in the mosque. Commencement of hostilities with the people of Mecca, the first blood shed, and the first booty taken by the Muslim.

Battle of Badr, or Bedr—a victory. January, A.D. 624.

A Surah, or chapter, issued about 'The Spoils,' how to be divided, which now forms Chapter VIII. of the Koran.

Commencement of disputes with the Jews, and the exile of the Benou Kainuka, a Jewish tribe settled at Madinah, to Syria.

Assassination of certain Jews.

Marriage of Muhammad to Hafsah, the daughter of Omar, on the death of her husband Khunais, December, A.D. 624. His fourth wife.

Defeat at Ohud, January, A.D. 625.

Further military expeditions.

The exile of the Benou Nadhir, another Jewish tribe residing near Madinah.

Muhammad marries a fifth wife, Zaineb-bint-

Khuzaimah, the widow of Obaidah, slain at Badr. January, A.D. 626.

Further hostilities with Arab tribes.

Muhammad marries his sixth wife, Omm-Salamah, widow of Abu Salamah, February, A.D. 626.

Further warlike expeditions.

Muhammad marries his seventh wife, Zainab bint Jahsh, purposely divorced by his freedman and adopted son Zaid bin Harithah, so that she might marry the Prophet. June, A.D. 626.

Further military expeditions.

Muhammad marries his eighth wife, Juwairiyyah-bint Harith, who survived him forty-five years. December, A.D. 626.

Ayesha, the favourite wife, and the daughter of Abu Bakr, accused of adultery, but eventually acquitted by a Divine revelation.

Siege of Madinah, February and March, A.D. 627.

Massacre of the Benou Koreitza, a Jewish tribe near Madinah. Muhammad takes Rohana, the beautiful Jewess, as a concubine.

Several minor expeditions.

An intended pilgrimage to Mecca, but Muhammad, with his followers, do not go further than Al-Hodeibiah.

A truce made with the Koraish for ten years, and permission given to Muhammad to visit the Kaabah the next year, for three days only. March, A.D. 628.

Letters sent by Muhammad to foreign sovereigns and princes, inviting them to embrace Islam; but these met with a moderate success only.

Expedition against the Jews of Khaibar, and its complete success. August, A.D. 628.

Marriage of Muhammad with Safiyyah, the bride of Kinanah, his ninth wife, August, A.D. 628. He partakes of a poisoned kid, dressed and offered to him by a woman named Zeinab.

His marriage with Omm Habiba, widow of Obaid Allah, and daughter of Abu Sofyan, October, A.D. 628. His tenth wife.

He takes Mary, the Coptic maid, as a concubine, sent to him by Jarih bin Mutta, the Governor of Egypt.

There were now nine wives and two concubines living in the harem of the Prophet.

Several small expeditions.

Despatch of further letters to foreign potentates and princes.

His pilgrimage to Mecca for three days, as previously stipulated, and known as the 'Solemn visit of the Fulfilment.' February, A.D. 629.

His marriage with Maimunah bint Harith, his eleventh and last wife.

Further important conversions at Mecca, such as Othman bin Talha, the guardian of the Kaabah; Amru, or Amr bin al-Aasi, a man renowned for sagacity, and who, during the Khalifate of Omar, conquered Egypt; and Khalid bin Walid, whose exploits obtained for him the title of 'The Sword of God.' This last was the most talented general of the Muslims.

Several military excursions.

Battle at Muta with certain Syrian tribes subject to the Roman authorities, September, A.D. 629. A defeat.

Further military expeditions.

Expedition against Mecca, and its complete success. Destruction of pictures, images, and idols at Mecca and the surrounding districts. January, A.D. 630.

Expedition against the Benou Thakif at Täif, and their allies the Benou Huwazin, and the battle of Honein, February, A.D. 630.

Siege of Täif, and its abandonment, followed later by the submission of Malik, the chief of the Benou Thakif, and the greater part of the tribe.

Muhammad performs the Lesser Pilgrimage and returns to Madinah.

The birth of a son by his Coptic slave and concubine Mary, April, A.D. 630. The boy, named Ibrahim, lived only about a year.

Quarrel with his legitimate wives about Mary, the Coptic slave, whom he had freed after the birth of the child.

Arrival of a Christian deputation at Madinah, and their discussions without conversion on either side. The Christians designated Jesus Christ as the Son of God, and the Second Person in the

Trinity. Muhammad denied this, quoting the following from the Koran :

'Jesus, the son of Mary, is only an apostle of God, and His word, which He conveyed into Mary, and a spirit proceeding from Himself. Believe, therefore, in God and His apostle, and say not three. Forbear; it will be better for you. God is only one God. Far be it from His glory that He should have a son.'

Deputations from certain Arab tribes.

Several lesser expeditions.

Campaign of Tabuk, which ended without fighting, and the submission of many tribes, October, A.D. 630.

Definite establishment of the Muslim Empire, A.D. 631.

Expedition of Ali to Yaman, December, A.D. 631.

Muhammad's solemn and greater pilgrimage to Mecca, i.e. 'the Al-Hijj,' or the Greater Pilgrimage, as compared with 'the Umrah,' or Lesser Pilgrimage. March, A.D. 632.

His speeches at this pilgrimage, known in Muhammadan history as 'The pilgrimage of the announcement,' or 'The pilgrimage of Islam,' or 'The farewell pilgrimage.' His establishment of the lunar year, and his farewell addresses.

Indisposition of Muhammad, and the three revolts—one headed by Tulaihah bin Khuwailid, a famous warrior of Najd; one by Musailamah; and one by Al-Aswad, all of which were eventually completely crushed after Muhammad's death by Abu Bakr and his generals.

Another expedition to Syria projected.

Muhammad's health becomes worse. His retirement to Ayesha's apartment. His final discourses.

Abu Bakr appointed to lead the public prayers.

Muhammad's last appearance in the mosque at Madinah.

His death and burial, June, A.D. 632.

From the above summary of the principal events of Muhammad's life, it will be perceived that up to the age of forty he was a student and acquirer of knowledge, much alone and occupied with his thoughts. At forty-one he began his public ministry, and stood forth as a reformer, preacher, and apostle at Mecca, and this continued till he finally left that place, in June, A.D. 622. As a reformer he proposed to do away with idols, to suppress gambling and drinking, and to abolish female infanticide, at that time much practised by the Arabs. As a preacher and apostle he urged the people to accept the belief in one God, whose injunctions were communicated to him by Gabriel for the benefit of the humanities. Prayer and ablution were also then ordained; fasting, almsgiving, and pilgrimages were instituted later on.

Before Muhammad's time there had been several earnest seekers after the one God, the God of Abraham. Of these persons Zaid, the Inquirer, may be mentioned, as also Warakah, a cousin of

Muhammad's first wife, Khadijah; Othman bin Huwairith, and Obaid Allah bin Jahsh. The people who professed this theism were termed Hanyfs; but their state of mind was as yet a purely speculative one, and they had announced nothing definite. But the ground was so far laid open, and had been prepared to a certain extent for Muhammad and his express revelation, that 'There was no God but the God, and that Muhammad was His apostle.'

It is highly probable that when Muhammad first began his public exhortations he had a strong idea of bringing not only the Arabs, but also the Jews and Christians, into his fold, and establishing one universal faith on the basis of one God, Almighty, Eternal, Merciful, Compassionate. It was on this account that he made Jerusalem the Kiblah, or consecrated direction of worship, and introduced into the Suras, or chapters, that he issued from time to time a good deal of matter connected with our Old and New Testaments. He particularly mentioned Abraham as the Father of the Faith, and acknowledging that there had already existed many thousand prophets, and three hundred and fifteen apostles, or messengers, he quoted nine of these last as special messengers, viz., Noah, Abraham, Jacob, Joseph, Moses, Job, David, Jesus, the son of Mary, and himself. To five of these he gave special titles. He called Noah the preacher of God; Abraham the friend of God;

Moses the converser with God; Jesus the spirit of God; and himself the apostle, or messenger, of God. But of the nine above mentioned four only, viz., Moses, David, Jesus, and Muhammad, held the highest rank as prophet-apostles.

It would, therefore, appear that Muhammad really hoped to establish one religion, acknowledging one God and a future life, and admitting that the earlier prophets had emanated from God as apostles or messengers. The world was too young and too ignorant in Muhammad's time to accept such an idea. It may, however, be accepted some day, when knowledge overcomes prejudice. Nations may have different habits, manners, and customs, but the God they all worship is one and the same.

Muhammad's life, from the age of forty to fifty, was one long struggle with the Koraish. Had it not been for the support given him by some of his influential relations at Mecca, he would either have been killed, or compelled to leave the place before he did. It is true that during these twelve years he made some excellent converts and faithful followers; but still it must be regarded as an historical fact that Muhammad failed at Mecca, as Jesus had failed at Jerusalem. In the one case Jesus was sacrificed, and passed away, leaving the story of His life, His words and His works in the heads of His disciples, who, with the suddenly converted Paul, certain Alexandrian Jews, the

Emperor Constantine, some literary remains of Plato, along with a destruction of adverse manuscripts and documents, finally established the Christian religion. In the other case Muhammad, failing at Mecca, succeeded at Madinah, and before his death had so far settled matters that the religion was fairly established, and was thus saved the severe and bitter struggles of the first centuries of the Christian Churches.

It has seldom been a matter of speculation as to what would have been the course of the world's history if Muhammad had been slain by the Koraish before he left Mecca, or if Jesus had not been crucified by the Jews. It is probable that in the end both religions would have been eventually established in other ways, and by other means, depending a good deal on the followers of the two men. But as the subject is purely speculative, it can hardly be entertained in this purely historical chapter.

Once at Madinah, Muhammad became a personage. Supported by his Meccan followers (al-Muhâjirûn), and the Madinese auxiliaries (Ansârs), he assumed immediately a spiritual and temporal authority, and became a sort of Pope-King. He kept that position for the rest of his life, improving it by his military successes, his diplomatic arrangements, his spiritual instructions, and his social legislation.

It was probably shortly before he went to

Madinah, or very soon after his arrival there, that he gave up all ideas of bringing over Jews, Christians, and Sabæans to his views. He determined to adapt them to the manners and customs of the Arabs only. In this he showed his wisdom and his knowledge of business. He changed the Kiblah from Jerusalem to Mecca. In the place of the Jewish trumpet, or the Christian bell, he introduced the call to prayer still heard from the tapering minarets of every mosque throughout the Muhammadan world.

By the Christian world it has been sometimes considered that Muhammad was good and virtuous at Mecca, but vicious and wicked at Madinah. Such calls to mind the reply of an Indian youth when asked in an examination to give an outline of the character of our good Queen Elizabeth. He briefly described her as 'a great and virtuous princess, but in her old age she became dissolute, and had a lover called Essex.'

But the position of Muhammad at Madinah was entirely different to what it had been at Mecca. At the latter place he was unable to assert himself. Indeed, it was as much as he could do to keep himself and his followers going at all, constantly subject as they were to persecution from the Koraish. All this was changed at Madinah, and his ten years' rule there was remarkable for his various military expeditions, his organization of the different tribes, his bitter persecution of the Jews, his still-continued inspired utterances, which now included spiritual, social, and legal matters, and his repeated marriages.

It has been frequently said that Muhammad, in his virtuous days, was content with one wife at Mecca, but in his vicious days at Madinah he had ten wives and two concubines. As a matter of fact, after Khadijah's death Muhammad's marriages were in most cases more or less a matter of business. By them he allied himself to Abu Bakr, Omar, Abu Sofyan, Khalid bin Walid, and other important persons. He further married the widows of some of his followers killed in battle, perhaps 'pour encourager les autres.' It is also probable that he was very anxious to have children, all of his having died except Fatima, who was married to Ali.

At the same time it must be admitted that Muhammad had a weakness for women in his later years—witness the case of Zainab bint Jahsh, the Jewish concubine Rohana, and the Coptic maid Mary. Indeed, his favourite wife Ayesha used to say of him: 'The Prophet loved three things— women, scents, and food; he had his heart's desire of the two first, but not of the last.' The reasons for this want of food, and many other traditions connected with the character of Muhammad, are to be found in the last chapter and the supplement at the end of Sir William Muir's most excellent and interesting work on the life of this extraordinary man, who, if author of the Koran only, would be entitled to rank among the immortals.

According to Muslim orthodox theology, the Koran is the inspired Word of God, uncreated, and eternal in its original essence. 'He who says the word of God is created is an infidel,' such is the decree of Muhammadan doctrine. Leaving everybody to form their own opinion on such a matter, it is only necessary here briefly to allude to the work, and to suppose that Muhammad was the inspired author of it.

The Koran is divided into 114 suras, or chapters, and 6,666 verses. The word itself signifies reading or recitation, and Muhammad always asserted that he only recited what had been repeated to him. But the Koran represents Muhammad from many points of view, in different capacities, and under different necessities. Ayesha, his favourite wife, when asked in later years as a widow to relate something about the Prophet, replied: 'Have you not the Koran, and have you not read it? for that will tell you everything about him.'

The Koran was not collected or arranged until after Muhammad's death. It is to be regretted that there is no reliable record of the exact order in which its various verses and chapters were given to the world by the Prophet, as that would have given us a great insight into the working of his mind from the time that he began his first recitals up to the time of his death. It is true that attempts have been made to formulate the order of delivery, but these can only be more or less conjecture. At the same time, though earlier and later verses appear mixed up in the different chapters, in some cases, of course, the period to which they belong can be pretty accurately fixed and determined.

As an interesting work, it can hardly be compared with our Old and New Testaments, nor would it be fair to make such a comparison. It must be remembered that the Koran is the work of Muhammad alone, while the Biblos, or Book, commonly called the Bible, is the work of many men. In its compilation many authors were rejected, and it represents as a whole the united talents of the ages. Indeed, the Bible may be considered as the most wonderful book in existence, and certainly the most interesting after visiting the countries it describes and the localities it refers to. If read from a matter-of-fact point of view, it gives an abundance of various kinds of literature, and describes the workings of the human mind from the earliest ages, and the progress of ideas as they gradually and slowly dawned upon man and drove him onwards. If read from a spiritual or mystical point of view, it can be interpreted in many ways to meet the views of either the readers or the hearers. In a word, the Bible is full of prose and poetry, fact and imagination, history and fiction.

It was lately described in an Italian newspaper, *Il Secolo*, about to issue a popular edition of it in halfpenny numbers, as follows :

'There is one book which gathers up the poetry and the science of humanity, and that book is the Bible; and with this book no other work in any literature can be compared. It is a book that Newton read continually, that Cromwell carried at his saddle, and that Voltaire kept always on his study table. It is a book that believers and unbelievers should alike study, and that ought to be found in every house.'

As a scientific work it has little value except that it represents the extent of scientific knowledge possessed by the authors at the time the different books were written.

To return to the Koran, which may, then, be regarded as the Bible of the Muslims. According to Mr. Badger : 'It embodies the utterances of the Arabian Prophet on all subjects, religious and moral, administrative and judicial, political and diplomatic, from the outset to the close of his career, together with a complete code of laws for regulating marriage, divorce, guardianship of orphans, bargains, wills, evidence, usury, and the intercourse of private and domestic life, as they were dictated by him to his secretaries, and by them committed to writing on palm-leaves, the shoulder-blades of sheep, and other tablets. These, it appears, were thrown pell-mell into chests, where they remained till the reign of Abu Bakr, the immediate successor of Muhammad, who, during the first year of his Khalifate, entrusted Zaid-bin Harithah, an Ansar, or auxiliary, and one of the amanuenses of the Prophet, with the task of collecting them together, which he did, as well from "the breasts of men" as from the afore-named materials, meaning thereby that he availed himself of the memories of those who had committed parts of the Prophet's utterances to memory. [Tradition states that one of the contemporary Muslims had learnt as many as seventy chapters by heart.] Zaid's copy continued to be the standard text during the Khalifate of Abu Bakr, who committed it to the keeping of Hafsah, one of Muhammad's widows. Certain disputes having arisen regarding this text, owing mainly to the variations of dialect and punctuation occurring therein, Omar, the successor of Abu Bakr, in the tenth year of his Khalifate, determined to establish a text which should be the sole standard, and delegated to Zaid, with whom he associated several eminent Arab scholars of the Al-Koraish, the task of its reduction. On its completion copies were forwarded to the principal stations of the empire, and all previously existing copies were submitted to the flames. This is the text now in general use among Muslims, and there is every reason to believe it to be a faithful rescript of the original fragmentary collection, amended only in its dialectical variations, and made conformable to the purer Arabic of the Al-Koraish, in which the contents of the Koran were announced by Muhammad.'

From a literary point of view the Koran is regarded as a specimen of the purest Arabic, and written in half poetry and half prose. It has been said that in some cases grammarians have adapted their rules to agree with certain phrases and expressions used in it, and that though several attempts have been made to produce a work equal to it, as far as elegant writing is concerned, none have as yet succeeded.

With the Koran, then, as a basis to work upon, Muhammad became the author and, it may be said, also founder of the Muhammadan faith, although as regards the foundation of any religion the followers of the author are generally the real founders of his faith. Of the three authors of great religions, viz., Moses, Buddha, and Jesus, who had gone before, Moses seems to have had much in common with Muhammad, and the two resembled each other in some ways. Buddha and Jesus were, on the other hand, entirely spiritualistic, their ideas on many subjects much the same, and their preachings and teachings run together very much on parallel lines.

The connecting links, however, between Buddhism and Christianity, if any, have yet to be discovered and determined. It may happen that some day further light may be thrown upon the subject; but at present, in spite of similarity of ideas, of sentiments, and of parables in the two religions, there is no positive proof of any connection between them, except that one preceded the other. While history has recorded every detail of Muhammad's life, both before and after his public ministry, which did not begin until he was forty years of age, history, alas! gives us no detailed record of the life of Jesus prior to the commencement of His public ministry in His thirtieth year. Had He travelled Himself to the further East? Had He studied under Buddhist missionaries? Had He taken the vows of poverty, chastity, and obedience, before He was baptized by John the Essene? Had He anything to do with the sects called Essenes, Therapeuts, Gnostics, Nazarites, the Brethren, which existed both before and during His lifetime? These, and many other questions which might be asked, can now probably never be answered, and the only thing that can be confidently asserted is that the character and the spiritual teachings of Christ, as handed down to us, much resemble the character and spiritual teachings of Buddha.

A few paragraphs must be devoted to Moses and Muhammad, as the first organizers of the Jews and the Arabs into separate and distinct nationalities. The two men had very different material to work upon, but they succeeded with the aid of Eloah, or Allah, supporting their own efforts.

It is probably historically true that the good old patriarch Abraham once lived, and may be considered to be the father of the Jewish, Christian, and Muhammadan religions. According to Arab tradition, Abraham, assisted by Ishmael, built the Kaabah at Mecca, so called because it was nearly a kaabah, or square. Anyhow, Abraham has ever been regarded with the greatest veneration by the Muslims, and his tomb at Hebron at the present day is so jealously guarded by them that the Jews and the Christians are not permitted to enter its sacred precincts.

Abraham and his followers worshipped Eloah, or the Almighty God, as the one and only God, offering up to Him at times various sacrifices. According to Rénan, in his 'History of the People of Israel,' 'the primitive religion of Israel was the worship of the Elohim, a collective name for the invisible forces that govern the world, and which are vaguely conceived as forming a supreme power at once single and manifold.'

'This vague primitive monotheism got modified during the migrations of the children of Israel, and especially during their struggles for the conquest of Palestine, and at last gave place to the conception of Jahveh, a national God conceived after the fashion of the gods of polytheism, essentially anthropomorphic, the God of Israel in conflict with the gods of the surrounding nations.'

'It was the task of the prophets to change this low and narrow conception of the Deity for a nobler one, to bring back the Jews to the Elohistic idea in a spiritualized form, and to transform the Jahveh or Jehovah of the times of the Judges into a God of all the earth—universal, one and absolute, that God in spirit and in truth of whom Jesus, the last of the prophets, completed the revelation.'

Certain events in the life of Joseph brought the family of Jacob to Egypt, separated it from the other tribes, and made the Israelites into a peculiar people.* As the twelve families of the sons of Jacob expanded into twelve tribes, they grew in number to such an extent that the Egyptian Government of the day began to be alarmed, and commenced coercive proceedings, which led to the appearance of Moses, first as a liberator, and then as the organizer of the twelve tribes into a Jewish nationality.

When Moses first took the children of Israel out of Egypt, it was probably his intention to lead them at once to the promised land. Finding, however, that their physical strength and courage was not equal to the conquest of Canaan, he kept them in the desert for forty years, until the open-air life and the hardy fare had produced a new generation of men fit to cope with the warriors of the land they were about to attempt to conquer.

Doubtless, during this residence in the desert

* The actual dates of these events and of the exodus from Egypt have not yet been historically fixed. How the Israelites first migrated to the land of Goshen, and how they eventually left Egypt, is still a question of considerable controversy. Further discoveries may yet throw further light on the subject.

Moses legislated both morally and socially for the Jews, as Muhammad did for the Arabs at Madinah. But as the Koran was not put together during Muhammad's life-time, so it is also highly probable that the Pentateuch, or five books of Moses, were not collected and collated till some time after his death, which last is described in the work itself.[*] Indeed, many things mentioned in them show a more advanced state of civilization than the children of Israel enjoyed during their wanderings in the desert.

But, still, to Moses the Jews owe their nationality, as the Arabs owed theirs to Muhammad. The former found a weak people, united to a certain extent, but quite unaccustomed to fighting and hardship, and he welded them sufficiently together to enable them, under his successors, to establish themselves in the promised land. The latter found Arabia inhabited by a quantity of tribes, more or less hostile to each other, but brave to a degree; fond of fighting and plundering, and always at it; full of local jealousies and internal enmities, which kept them separate. Muhammad not only induced them to believe in one God, but also brought them together to such an extent that his successors were able to launch them as united warriors and conquerors throughout the East, and to found an

[*] This subject is treated at considerable length by Dr. A. Kuenen in 'The Religion of Israel,' translated by Alfred Heath May from the Dutch. Williams and Norgate: London, 1882.

empire for the time being far greater, grander, and more important than Canaan, as divided among the twelve tribes, or the dominions of David and Solomon.

As a military leader Muhammad was not particularly celebrated. The military expeditions undertaken by him in person are variously stated to have been from nineteen to twenty-seven in number, whilst those in which he was not present are stated to have amounted to more than fifty. With the exception of one or two to the Syrian frontier, they were chiefly directed against the Arabs and the Jews in Arabia, but none of them were of the magnitude of those undertaken by his successors, Abu Bakr and Omar, who, with the aid of the generals Khalid, son of Walid, Mothanna, Amr bin Al'Aasi, and others, made great conquests, and finally established the Muslim faith on a firm and lasting basis. The details of these successes are admirably told in Muir's 'Annals of the Early Khalifate.'

There appears to be a great resemblance between many of the military and warlike expeditions undertaken by Muhammad in Arabia, and those of the Jews, as narrated in the historical works of the Old Testament, in Palestine. In both countries God was used as the authority, and individuals and tribes were attacked and slaughtered much in the same way. Indeed, if the numbers slain, as recorded by the Jewish historians, are to be depended upon, it can only be inferred that the God of the Jews was more vindictive and bloodthirsty than the God of the Arabs. At the present time the Soudanese and their Khalifahs seem to be following very much in the steps of Muhammad, constantly sending forth military expeditions, and issuing letters to foreign potentates.

In conclusion, the dogmas and precepts of Islam, as embodied in the Koran, may be summed up as follows :

(1) Belief in Allah or God, or, more correctly, 'The God;' that is, the only God. ' Al,' the ; ' Ilah,' a God.

(2) Belief in the Messengers or Angels.

(3) Belief in the Books or Scriptures, and in the Prophets.

(4) Belief in Hell and Paradise.

(5) Belief in a general resurrection and final judgment.

(6) Belief in the decrees of God, or of His having absolutely predestined both good and evil.

The five cardinal ordinances of Islam are :

(1) The pious recitation of the Kalimah, or Creed: ' There is no God but the one God, and Muhammad is his Apostle.'

(2) Prayer.

(3) Fasting.

(4) Legal and obligatory almsgiving.

(5) Pilgrimage.

There are several other points connected with the institutions of Islam, such as—
(1) Circumcision.
(2) Marriage and polygamy.
(3) Slavery.
(4) The Jihad, or Holy War.
(5) Food, drink and ablutions.

But full details connected with the above will be found, if required, in Hughes' 'Dictionary of Islam,' so that further reference to them here is unnecessary. It must, however, always be remembered that faith and prayer were the two points which Muhammad always insisted upon as absolutely essential.

The Muhammadan religion may be regarded as creating in theory the purest democracy in existence. All men are supposed to be equal. There are no hereditary titles. Every man can rise, either by interest or talent, from the very lowest to the very highest position. There is a universal feeling of brotherhood among the Muslims. All this is excellent in theory, but in practice the ways of the world are different. A Pasha holds his place and upholds his position, while a humble follower of the said Pasha, or other person in an inferior position, knows his place also, and treats his superiors and his inferiors accordingly. In fact, both in the East and the West there appears to be a place for all men, and that place is established by the unwritten laws of the world or by the law of nature, in spite of the many theories propounded by religion, politics, or political economy. Still, Muhammad himself instilled equality among his followers, and in his parting address at Mina, at the time of the farewell pilgrimage, spoke as follows:

'Ye people! hearken to my speech and comprehend the same. Know that every Muslim is the brother of every other Muslim. All of you are on the same equality' (and as he pronounced these words he raised his arms aloft and placed the forefinger of one hand on the forefinger of the other, intending thereby to signify that all were absolutely on the same level); 'ye are one brotherhood.

'Know ye what month this is? What territory is this? What day?' To each question the people gave the appropriate answer, viz.:

'The sacred month, the sacred territory, the great day of pilgrimage.' After every one of these replies Muhammad added:

'Even thus sacred and inviolable hath God made the life and the property of each of you unto the other, until ye meet your Lord.

'Let him that is present tell it unto him that is absent. Haply, he that shall be told may remember better than he who hath heard it.'

CHAPTER IV.

TALES AND STORIES.

OF the two hundred and fifty books of tales, the titles of which are given in the 'Fihrist,' only three or four have attained European fame. Firstly, the book known in Arabic as 'Kalilah wa Dimnah,' containing the celebrated Indian apologues, or the so-called fables of Bidpay, on the origin of which several dissertations have been written.

In 'Early Ideas' (W. H. Allen and Co., 1881) mention was made of the fables of Bidpay, or Pilpai, as being the traditionally oldest-known collection of stories in Hindustan, and that from them the 'Pancha Tantra,' or 'Five Chapters,' and the 'Hitopodesa,' or 'Friendly Advice,' are supposed to have been drawn.

In 'Persian Portraits' (Quaritch, 1887) it was noted that the Persian work called 'Kalilah wa Dimnah' is said to have been originally derived from the fables of Bidpay, and that it led to the longer and larger works known in Persian literature as the 'Anwar-i-Suheli,' or 'The Lights of

Canopos,' and the 'Ayar-Danish,' or 'The Touchstone of Knowledge.'

It is highly probable that this work of 'Kalilah wa Dimnah' (translated from Persian into Arabic by Ibn Al-Mukaffa about A.D. 750), and another Persian work, not now extant, but known as the 'Hazar Afsaneh,' or 'Thousand Stories,' were the first sources from which were commenced to be compiled the best collection of tales and stories in Arabic literature, and called 'The Thousand and One Nights,' and popularly known in this country as 'The Arabian Nights.'

As regards the 'Hazar Afsaneh,' or 'Thousand Stories,' it is much to be regretted that all trace of this work has disappeared. It is, however, mentioned by Masudi, and An-Nadim, the author of the 'Fihrist,' but whether they had actually seen and perused the whole work is uncertain. It may have been completed during the rule of the Sasanian dynasty in Persia (A.D. 228-641), some of whose kings were patrons of letters, and the work, or portions of it, may have been destroyed along with a large quantity of other Persian literature at the time of the conquest of the Persian Empire by the Arabs in A.D. 641. At all events, it has not yet been found, though it is still hoped that it may turn up some day.

As regards the 'Nights' themselves, it is impossible to fix any exact date to them, neither can they be ascribed to any particular authors. From the book as it has come down to us, there is ample evidence to assert that the collection of all the tales and stories occupied many years, and that the authors of them were numerous. As great progress was made in Arab literature from the commencement of the rule of the Abbaside dynasty in A.D. 750, it may be inferred that the work itself dates from that period, and that it had been put together in a certain form before the fall of Baghdad in A.D. 1258. After that date other stories were probably added, and the whole répertoire was perhaps put together again in its present shape either at Cairo or Damascus, with numerous alterations and additions.

It is believed that the fables and apologues are the oldest part of the book. These bear on their face a decided impress of the Farther East; indeed, they are quite of the nature of the stories told in the 'Pancha Tantra,' 'Kathá Sarit Ságara,' 'Hitopodesa,' and 'Kalilah wa Dimnah,' many of them being either the same, or bearing a very great resemblance to them. Animal fables generally may have originated in India, where the doctrine of metempsychosis obtains currency to this day; but, still, Egypt, Greece, and other countries, have also produced stories of the same nature. From the time of the early Egyptians, the fable has ever been the means of conveyance of both instruction and amusement to mankind. And as years rolled by the fable grew into the tale or story, which later on expanded into the romance and the novel.

After the fables the oldest tales in the 'Nights' are supposed to be the Sindibad, or the tale of the king, his son, his concubine, and the seven wazirs; and that of King Jali'ad of Hind, and his wazir Shimas, followed by the history of King Wird Khan, son of King Jali'ad, with his women and wazirs. These tales have also an Indian flavour about them, both with regard to the animal stories in them and to the sapient remarks about the duties of kings and their ministers, often referred to in the Kathá Sarit Ságara, of which more anon.

The remaining tales and stories in the 'Nights' may be of Persian, Arabian, Egyptian, and Syrian origin, some earlier and some later. The adventures of Kamar Al-Zaman and the jeweller's wife, and of Ma'aruf, the cobbler, and his wife Fatimah, are considered to be two of the very latest stories, having been assigned to the sixteenth century. The story of Aboukir, the dyer, and Abousir, the barber, is quoted by Payne 'as the most modern of the whole collection.'

Certain stories of the 'Nights' were first introduced to Europe, between 1704-1708, by Antoine Galland, a Frenchman, whose biography is given by Burton in his 'Terminal Essay,' vol. x., and most interesting it is. The work of the translation of Arabic and Persian stories was continued by Petis de la Croix (1710-12), Morell (1765), Dow

(1768), Chavis and Cazotte (1787-89), Caussin de Perceval (1806), Gauttier (1822), Jonathan Scott (1811), Von Hammer Purgstall (1823), Zinzerling (1823-24), Trebutien (1828), Habicht (1825-39), Weil (1838-42), Torrens (1838), Lane (1838-40), and the 'Nights' themselves have now been completely finished by John Payne (1882-84) and Richard Burton (1885-88).

A perusal of the productions of all the translators above mentioned will show that, as regards finality, both Payne and Burton have done their work completely, thoroughly, and exhaustively, and for all time, as far as an English translation is concerned. Too much credit cannot be given to these two gentlemen for their untiring labour and energy. The more the 'Nights' are read, the more will people appreciate the amount of hard work and acumen, intelligence and ability, which has been thrown into the undertaking by these two accomplished littérateurs. And it is highly probable that their translations, along with Galland's volumes in French, will ever remain as the standard European versions of this great series of Oriental tales.

Space will not permit of a lengthy description of all that is contained in Payne's thirteen, and in Burton's sixteen, volumes. To be appreciated thoroughly, they must be read, like Balzac's works, from the very beginning to the very end. At the same time a brief analysis of these two translations of the 'Nights' may perhaps be interesting, and will serve the purposes of the present chapter.

The first nine of Payne's, and the first ten of Burton's, volumes are devoted to the 'Nights' proper, and follow the same lines. The translation has been made from what are commonly known as the Boulac (Cairo) and the two Calcutta Arabic texts of the 'Nights,' though references are made to the Breslau (Tunis) edition, from which also some extracts have been taken and some translations made. The contents of these volumes may be divided into four heads ;

(1) Fables and apologues.

(2) Short stories and anecdotes, some biographical and historical.

(3) Tales and stories.

(4) Long stories, or romances.

Excluding the two short stories in the introductory chapter, there are 10 principal and 6 subordinate fables under the first heading, 116 principal and 3 subordinate stories under the second, 38 principal and 75 subordinate under the third, and 6 principal and 12 subordinate under the fourth heading. This gives a total of 170 principal and 96 subordinate stories in Burton's edition, while Payne gives one principal story and one subordinate one less, his numbers being 169 and 95 respectively. By principal is meant the main or chief story, while by subordinate is meant another story forming part of the main story. In Oriental literature this custom is frequently introduced. A story is commenced, but owing to some allusion in it another story is interpolated, and when this is finished, the original tale is reverted to, only, perhaps, to be interpolated again by another story, and so on.

Out of this mass of fable, tale and story, it is difficult to select any particular ones that may prove interesting to everybody. Some are very good, others good, some fairish, and others indifferent; but all are more or less interesting, as they deal with all sorts and conditions of men and women, and all sorts of events and situations. Personally, some twelve stories have struck me as particularly interesting or amusing, though it does not at all follow that what one person fancies another person cares about. A perusal of the work itself will enable its readers to find out what they like for themselves, while the following brief remarks on the twelve stories alluded to above will give a scanty outline of them.

The tale of Aziz and Azizah is one of the best in the whole collection. It represents the care and fondness of a truly loving woman, who did her best to shield and protect her very stupid cousin. It is said that people marry for three reasons, viz., for love, for money, or for protection. In truth, nobody can protect a man from a woman as another woman. No man can drive off a woman, divine her intention, or insult her so violently as a woman can, and this is generally understood both in the East and West. In the present story, Azizah first helps her cousin Aziz to woo and win, endeavouring to shield and protect him at the same time from this daughter of Dalilah, the wily one. Had it not been for Azizah's good advice and farewell saying of ' Faith is fair, and unfaith is foul,' Aziz would have surely perished. Eventually, the loving Azizah dies of a broken heart.

Aziz, though repeatedly warned by his mistress, the daughter of Dalilah, not to have anything to do with the sex on account of his youth and simplicity, falls into the hands of another woman, who first marries him, and then keeps him locked up in her house, and never lets him out for a whole year. When, however, he does get away for a day only, he goes at once to see his former mistress, who is furious on hearing that he is married to somebody else, and with the aid of her slave girls serves him out in a way which, from one point of view, makes marriage quite a failure for him in the future. On going back to his wife, she, having found out what had occurred, immediately puts him into the street, and he returns in a sad plight to his mother, who nurses him and gives him the present and the letter that his cousin Azizah had left for him. Finally Aziz, for the sake of distraction, takes to foreign travel, and there meets with Taj al Muluk, whom he assists to find the princess Dunya.

The tale of Kamar Al-Zaman and the Lady

Budur is both amusing and interesting. It is truly an Eastern story, full of curious and wonderful situations, and quite a kaleidoscope of passing events, which succeed each other rapidly. The hero and the heroine are a young prince and princess, living in very different parts of the world (space and geography have no place in the 'Nights'), and both very averse to matrimony. The one fears the smiles and wiles of woman, the other the tyranny and selfishness of man. A certain Queen of the Jinns, with her assistants, bring the two together one night in the same bed, and separate them in the morning. But the sight that each had had of the other caused them to fall desperately in love, and deep are the lamentations of each over the separation, which continues for some years. At last Kamar Al-Zaman finds his way to his lady-love, the Princess Budur, and they are happily wedded; alas! after a short time, to be again separated. Then follow the adventures of each — the lady becomes a king, and is married to a princess, and rules a country, while Kamar Al-Zaman's fate assigns him the place of an under-gardener. Destiny, however, re-unites them, and the Lady Budur's joke before recognition and re-union is certainly humorous. She makes him further marry the lady that she herself was married to, and a son is born to each, respectively called Amjad and Asaad. When the boys grow up, the mother of each falls violently in love with the son of the other, *i.e.*, Budur adores Asaad, and Heyat en Nufus worships Amjad, and the two mothers end by making dishonourable proposals to the two sons. These overtures being indignantly rejected, the mothers, as in all Eastern tales, turn the tables by informing their husband that his sons had made indecent proposals to them. In consequence they are sent off to be slain in the desert, but, from the circumstances which occur there, the executioner spares their lives, and returns with their clothes steeped in a lion's blood, reporting that he has carried out the king's instructions, and quoting their last message to their father :

'Women are very devils, made to work us dole and death ;
 Refuge I seek with God Most High from all their craft and skaith.
 Prime source are they of all the ills that fall upon mankind,
 Both in the fortunes of this world and matters of the faith.'

The king at once recognises their innocence, and mourns over their loss, building two tombs in their memory, called the Houses of Lamentations, where he spends his days weeping.

Meanwhile the two youths, left to their own devices by the executioner, journey onward, arrive at a city, become separated, go through all sorts of adventures, all of a most thrilling description, and are finally re-united. The closing scene brings all the characters of the romance together at the same place, and the grandfathers, fathers, and sons all meet once more, but no further mention is made about the two mothers, who so deeply injured their own offspring.

Ala Aldin Abu Al-Shamat.—This story is of considerable interest, for it begins with a recipe for an aphrodisiac, and contains many allusions to Eastern manners and customs. Born of wealthy parents at Cairo, details are given of Ala Aldin's youth and boyhood, and of how the wish to travel and to trade was instilled into his mind by his young companions, at the instigation of a crafty old sinner, Mahmud of Balkh. With some reluctance his father at last allows him to start, and going first to Damascus, then to Aleppo, he is robbed of all his property just before he reaches Baghdad, and very nearly loses his life into the bargain, but his good fortune saves him on two occasions. Arrived at Baghdad, his adventures begin, and they follow each other with considerable rapidity. He first is married to Zobeidah the Lutist, on the understanding that it was for one night only, and that he was to divorce her the next morning, so that she might be re-married to her former husband. But when the time comes, Ala Aldin and the lady find each other such pleasant company that they absolutely decline to divorce, and elect to pay the fine. This money is provided for them by Harun-ar-Rashid, who visits them one night with three of his companions all disguised as dervishes, and they are charmed with

Zobeidah's performance on the lute, her singing, and her recitations.

Ala Aldin then goes to the Court, where he rises to high favour and receives various good appointments. To his great grief he loses his wife, who dies, as he supposes, and is buried with the usual mourning, but in reality turns up again at the end of the tale, and is re-united to her husband. It appears that a servant of the Jinn had carried her off to another country, leaving a Jinneyah to be buried in her place.

To make up for the loss of Zobeidah, the Khalif gives Ala Aldin one of his own slave-girls, Kut al Kulub by name, and sends her, with all her belongings, to his house. Ala Aldin will not have anything to do with her, on the grounds—'What was the master's should not become the man's;' but he lodges, boards, and treats her handsomely. Eventually Harun takes her back, and orders a slave-girl to be bought at his expense in the market for ten thousand dinars for Ala Aldin. This is done, and a girl named Jessamine is purchased and given to him. He sets her at once free and marries her.

But at the time of the purchase another man had been bidding for this same girl, and, being much in love with her, his family determine to assist him in getting hold of her. A whole lot of fresh characters then appear on the scene, and, after much plotting and intrigue, Ala Aldin is arrested and sentenced to death. He, however, escapes to Alexandria, and there opens a shop. Further adventures follow, till he finds himself at Genoa, where he remains for some time as servant in a church. Meanwhile at Baghdad his wife Jessamine has borne him a son, named Asdan, who grows up, and in time discovers the author and nature of the theft of which his father had been accused, and thus prepares the way for his return to the city of the Khalifs. This is brought about by the Princess Husn Maryam at Genoa, with whom Ala Aldin finds his first wife Zobeidah, and they all set out on a wonderful couch and go first to Alexandria, then to Cairo to visit his parents, and finally to Baghdad, where he marries the princess and lives happy ever afterwards.

Ali the Persian and the Kurd Sharper is a very short story, but quite Rabelaisian in its humour, and the manner in which the Persian and the Kurd describe the contents of the small bag that had been lost. All sorts of things are mentioned in a haphazard way, many of them, however, perhaps, being required to fulfil the exigencies of the rhymed prose in which the story is written in the original Arabic.

The Man of Al-Yaman and his six Slave-Girls.— The six girls in this story have all different qualities. One is white, another brown, the third fat, the fourth lean, the fifth yellow, and the sixth black. The happy owner gets them together, and in verse and recitation each praises her own peculiarity, and abuses that of her opposite by examples and quotations. There is an Oriental twang about the story which makes it worthy of notice, and some of the verses are not bad.

Abu Al-Husn and his slave-girl Tawaddud.— This story is not amusing, but it is very interesting, especially to persons studying the minute details of the Muhammadan faith, doctrine and practice, according to the Shafai school, and the exegesis of the Koran, all of which are wonderfully expounded by the slave-girl. In the shape of questions and answers an enormous amount of information of all sorts is put into the mouth of this highly accomplished female. The writer deals not only with theology, but also with physiology in all its branches, or, at least, with as many as were known at the period of the tale. Further, medicine, astronomy, philosophy, and all kinds of knowledge are discussed. A series of conundrums are put to the girl and replied to by her, and she also displays her skill in chess, draughts, backgammon, and music.

It is to be regretted that the exact date of this species of Mangnall's Questions and Answers cannot be ascertained, for this would enable us to appreciate better the amount of knowledge displayed on the various subjects under discussion. Anyhow, it is certain that it must have been written some time after the doctrines of the Imam Shafai (he died

A.D. 820) had been well-defined and established. Owing to certain medical and surgical queries and replies, it is to be presumed that the whole must have been worked up after the Arab school of medicine and physiology had arrived at their highest stage of perfection. The whole story is a good specimen of the state of civilization reached by the Arabs, and as such is worth a reference.

Three other stories in the 'Nights' bear some affinity to the above, but they are much more limited, both as regards the subject they deal with and the information they supply. One is 'King Jali'ad and his vizier Shimas,' in Payne's eighth and Burton's ninth volume; another, 'History of Al-Hajjaj bin Yusuf and the young Sayyid,' in Burton's fifth supplemental; and the third, 'The Duenna and the King's Son,' in his sixth supplemental.

The Rogueries of Dalilah the Crafty, and her daughter, Zeynab the Trickstress.—The tricks played by Dalilah the Crafty on all sorts of people in this story are of a nature that would make the tale amusing to the Arabs generally, and to the frequenters of coffee-houses particularly. Dalilah's father and husband had held lucrative appointments under the Khalifs of Baghdad, and, with a view to obtain something for herself and her daughter Zeynab, these two women determined to bring themselves to notice by playing tricks, and doing things which were likely to be talked of in the great city. In Europe at the present time the same method is often followed. Attempted assassinations, attempted suicides, complaints in the police-courts and cases in the law-courts are sometimes meant simply as an advertisement.* Anyhow, Dalilah's tricks played on various people are certainly amusing, and as they run ingeniously one into the other, it is somewhat difficult to describe them in a few words. The tale, to be appreciated, must be read through. Sufficient to add that Dalilah and Zeynab both eventually obtain what they wish, and the various things taken from the different parties are duly returned to them.

The Adventures of Quicksilver Ali of Cairo.—This story is of the same nature as the preceding one, and in all the editions of the 'Nights' the one always follows the other, while in the Breslau

---

* As an example take the following extract from the *Daily Telegraph* of 16th July, 1889:

'The sisters Macdonald have been giving a great deal more trouble to the police lately than even the bearers of so historic a name are entitled to give. Ethel Macdonald appeared at Marlborough Street charged with having wilfully smashed a window at the Junior Carlton Club, St. James's Square. It was stated that the aggressive Ethel was one of the daughters of an ex-superintendent of county constabulary deceased, and that his daughters, being left unprovided for, had taken to going on the "rampage." One of the sisters alleges that she has been wronged by "a rich man," and a short time since another Miss Macdonald, on being arraigned before Mr. Newton, flung a bottle at the head of that learned magistrate. Ethel was discharged, but it was ordered that she should be sent to the workhouse for inquiries to be made into her state of mind.'

text the two stories run together. Ali begins life at Cairo, and ends at Baghdad, where his tricks and adventures follow each other in rapid succession, his object being to obtain in marriage the hand of Zeynab, the daughter of Dalilah the Crafty. He is first tricked himself by Zeynab, but continues his pursuit of her, and though at times he is transformed into the shapes of an ass, a bear, and a dog by the magic arts of Azariah the Jew, eventually he succeeds, with the aid of the Jew's daughter, in obtaining the property required, and finally marries Zeynab, the Jewess, and two other women.

Hasan of Busra and the King's Daughter of the Jinn.—This is a good specimen of a real Oriental romance, with the wonderful and marvellous adventures of the hero interlaced with magic, alchemy, the Jinns, and other fabulous varieties, so that the highest ideals of the imagination are almost arrived at.

Bahram the Magician, who first beguiles Hasan with alchemy and then carries him off and endeavours to destroy him, is himself destroyed in the early part of the story. The kindness of the seven princesses to Hasan during his stay with them, and his visits to them later on, are described at length, as also is the way in which the hero falls desperately in love with the king's daughter of the Jinn, and secures her as his bride. The happy pair start for Busra, and rejoin his mother, and then settle down in Baghdad, where two sons are born and happiness reigns supreme. But during Hasan's absence on a visit to his former friends the seven princesses, some domestic scenes between his wife, his mother, and Zobeidah, the spouse of the Khalif Harun-ar-Rashid, are introduced, which end by the wife re-possessing herself of her original feather garment, and flying off with her two children to the islands of Wac, where her father and family resided.

On his return Hasan is broken-hearted to find her gone, and determines to set out and try and recover her. Then follows the description of his journeys, which fill pages describing the white country, and the black mountain, the land of camphor, and the castle of crystal. The islands of Wac were seven in number, peopled by Satans and Marids, and warlocks and tribesmen of the Jinn. To reach them Hasan has to traverse the island of birds, the land of beasts, and the valley of Jinn. Without the aid of the princesses, their uncle Abdul-cuddous, Abourruweish, Dehnesh ben Feetesh, Hassoun, king of the land of Camphor, and the old woman Shawahi, he never would have reached his destination. This, however, he finally does, and with the aid of a magic cup and wand recovers his wife and children, and returns with them to Baghdad, where they live happily ever afterwards, till there came to them the Creditor whose debt must always be paid sooner or later, the Destroyer of delights, and the Severer of societies.

Ali Nur Al-din and Miriam the Girdle-Girl (called by Payne, the Frank King's Daughter).— The adventures of Ali with Miriam, whom he first buys as a slave-girl in Alexandria, and from whom he is separated and re-united, again separated and again united, are told at some length. But the principal features in this tale are the innumerable verses in praise of various fruits, flowers, wine, women, musical instruments, the beauty of the hero, etc., and on the subjects of love, union, separation, etc. Miriam herself is a charming character of self-reliance and independence. On her first appearance in the slave market, at the time of her sale, she declines to be purchased by the old men, and abuses their age and their infirmities. Indeed, she seemed to be of the same opinion as our great national poet, who wrote :

'Crabbed age and youth
Cannot live together;
Youth is full of plaisance,
    Age is full of care;
Youth like summer morn,
Age like winter weather;
Youth like summer brave,
    Age like winter bare.
Youth is full of sport,
Age's breath is short,
    Youth is nimble, age is lame;
Youth is hot and bold,
Age is weak and cold,
    Youth is wild and age is tame.

Age, I do abhor thee;
Youth, I do adore thee;
  O my love, my love is young;
Age, I do defy thee,
O sweet shepherd, hie thee,
  For methinks thou stay'st too long.'

However, she finally consents to be bought by the young and good-looking Ali, who spends his last thousand dinars in her purchase, and then has nothing to live upon. Miriam remedies this by making every night a beautiful girdle, which Ali sells for a good price in the bazaar next day. This goes on for upwards of a year, when the first separation is brought about by the crafty old Wazir of her father, the King of France, who had sent him especially to look for his daughter. In the course of the adventures that follow, Miriam shows her capacity in sailing ships and in killing various men, among others her three brothers, who pursued her in her last flight from her father's city. Eventually she and Ali get to Baghdad, where the Khalif makes things smooth for them, and they are married, and finally return to Cairo to rejoin Ali's parents, from whom he had run away in his youth.

Kamar Al-Zaman and the Jeweller's Wife is one of the modern tales of the 'Nights,' and a very good one, containing a good plot and plenty of interesting incidents. The jeweller's wife, Halimah by name, is one of the wickedest and craftiest of women in Busra, and her plots and intrigues are well described; some of them are to be found in Persian story-books. After playing all sorts of tricks, she leaves her husband, and elopes with the youth Kamar to Cairo, where his parents reside. There his father will not let him marry her, but confines her and her slave-girl in a room, and arranges a marriage for his son with another woman. After a time Halimah's husband, Obayd, the jeweller, turns up in Cairo in the most beggarly plight, having been plundered by Bedouins *en route*. After explanations, Obayd ends by killing his wife and her slave-girl, who had assisted her in all her devilries, and Kamar's father marries him to his daughter, who turns out the most virtuous of women. The moral of the tale is pointed out at the end, that there are both bad women and good women in the world, and is closed with the remark: 'So he who deemeth all women to be alike, there is no remedy for the disease of his insanity.'

Ma'aruf the Cobbler and his wife Fatimah commences with a domestic scene between the two, from which it appears that the poor husband had been shamefully sat upon from the day of his marriage, and that his wife was a dreadful woman. Affairs, however, at last reach a climax, and Ma'aruf seeks peace and safety in flight. Balzac, in his clever novel of 'Le Contrat de Mariage,' makes his hero Manerville fly from the machinations of his wife and mother-in-law, but Henri de Marsay, writing to his friend pages on the subject, contends that he is wrong, and points out to him the course that he should have followed. Anyhow, in Ma'aruf the Cobbler's case, the result is satisfactory. Arriving by the aid of a Jinn at a far-away city, he found a friend, who directed him how to behave, and to tell everybody that he was a great and wealthy merchant, but that his merchandise was still on the way, and expected daily. Pending the arrival of his baggage-train, Ma'aruf borrowed from everybody, gave it all away in largesse to the poor, and behaved generally as if he were very well-to-do. By these means he made such an impression on the King of the place that the latter married him to his daughter, and made large advances from the treasury in anticipation of the arrival of the merchandise.

Time goes on, but still the baggage does not turn up. The King, instigated by his Wazir, becomes suspicious, and persuades his daughter to worm out the real story from her husband. This she does in a clever way, and Ma'aruf tells her his true history. The woman behaves admirably, refuses to expose his vagaries, and, giving him fifty thousand dinars, advises him to fly to a foreign country, to begin to trade there, and to keep her informed of his whereabouts and the turn of his fortunes. The Cobbler departs during the night, while his wife the next morning tells the King and the Wazir a long rigmarole story of how her husband had been summoned by his servants, who had informed him that his baggage-train and merchandise had been attacked by the Arabs, and that he had gone himself to look after his affairs.

Meanwhile Ma'aruf departs sore at heart, weeping bitterly, and, like all 'Arabian Nights' heroes in adversity, repeating countless verses. After various adventures he falls in with a vast treasure, and a casket containing a seal ring of gold, which, when rubbed, causes the slave of the seal ring, naturally a Jinn, to appear and carry out every wish and order that Ma'aruf might give him. With the aid, then, of the Jinn, Abu Al-Saddat by name, the Cobbler returns to his wife laden with treasure and merchandise, and thus proves to all the doubters that he is a true man. He pays all his debts, gives a great deal to the poor, and bestows presents of an enormous value on his wife, her attendants, and all the people of the Court.

As a matter of course, all this prosperity is followed by adversity. The King and his Wazir combine together, and ask Ma'aruf to a garden-party, make him drunk, and get him to relate the story of his success. Recklessly he shows the ring to the Wazir, who gets hold of it, rubs it, and on the appearance of the slave of the ring, orders him to carry off the Cobbler and cast him down in the desert. The Wazir then orders the King to be treated in the same way, while he himself seizes the Sultanate, and aspires to marry Ma'aruf's wife, the King's daughter.

With much interesting detail the story relates how the Princess Dunya gets the ring into her possession, sends the Wazir to prison, and rescues her father and her husband from the desert. The Wazir is then put to death, and the ring is kept by the lady, as she thinks it would be safer in her keeping than in that of her relations. After this a son is born, the King dies, Ma'aruf succeeds to the throne, and shortly after loses his wife, who before her death gives him back the ring, and urges him to take good care of it for his own sake and for the sake of his boy.

Time goes on, and the Cobbler's first wife, Fatimah, turns up in town, brought there also by a Jinn, and tells the story of the want and suffering she had undergone since his departure from Cairo. Ma'aruf treats her generously, and sets her up in a palace with a separate establishment, but the wickedness of the woman reappears, and she tries to get hold of the ring for her own purposes. Just as she has secured it she is cut down and killed on the spot by Ma'aruf's son, who had been watching her proceedings, and is thus finally disposed of. The King and his son then marry, and live happily in the manner of Eastern story, all the other characters being properly provided for.

So much for the 'Nights' proper. Other stories translated from the Breslau text (a Tunisian manuscript acquired, collated and translated by Professor Habicht, of Breslau, Von der Hagen, and another; 15 volumes, 12mo., Breslau, 1825), the Calcutta fragment of 1814-1818, and other sources, have been given by Payne in three extra volumes entitled 'Tales from the Arabic,' and by Burton in two of his six volumes of the 'Supplemental Nights.' Payne's three books and Burton's two first volumes follow the same lines. They both contain twenty principal, and sixty-four subordinate stories, or eighty-four altogether, divided into nine short stories and seventy-five longer ones. Some of them are very interesting, and some are amusing, especially a few of the sixteen Constables' Stories, which describe the cleverness of women, and the adroitness of thieves, and people of that class. It is probable that these are more or less of a modern date.

The first story in this collection, called 'The Sleeper and the Waker,' commonly known as 'The Sleeper Awakened,' is good, and also particularly interesting as one of Galland's stories not traced at the time, but afterwards turning up in the Tunis text of the 'Nights.'

The third volume of Burton's 'Supplemental Nights' is one of the most interesting of the whole lot. It contains eight principal and four subordinate stories of Galland's 'Contes Arabes,' which are not included in the Calcutta, Boulak, or Breslau editions of the 'Nights.' For many years the sources from which Galland procured these tales were unknown. Some said that he invented them himself. Others conjectured that he got them from the story-tellers in Constantinople and other places in the East. But in A.D. 1886 Mr. H. Zotenberg, the keeper of Eastern Manuscripts in the Bibliothèque Nationale at Paris, obtained a manuscript copy of the 'Nights,' which contained the Arabic originals of the stories of 'Zayn Al Asnam,' and of 'Aladdin,' two of Galland's best stories. This was a very valuable acquisition, for it sets at rest the doubts that had always been expressed about the origin of these two tales, and also leads to the supposition that the Arabic originals of the other stories will also turn up some day.

Of these eight principal and four subordinate stories of Galland, those of 'Aladdin; or, The Wonderful Lamp,' and of 'Ali Baba and the Forty Thieves,' have ever been most popular tales, and have been appreciated by many generations from the time that Galland first introduced them to Europe. But some of the other stories are equally good, and all are worth reading, as Burton has not only taken Galland as a guide, but has also adapted his own translation from the Hindustani version of the Gallandian tales, prepared by one Totárám Shayán, whose texts of the 'Nights,' along with those of others, are fully discussed. By this method Burton endeavoured to preserve the

Oriental flavour of the work itself, without introducing too much French sauce.

After the discovery of the Arabic original of the stories of ' Zayn Al-Asnam ' and ' Aladdin,' Payne recognized its importance, and published his translation of these two tales in a separate volume in 1889, which forms a sort of appendix to his previously issued twelve volumes. This thirteenth book contains also an interesting introduction, giving a *résumé* of Mr. Zotenberg's work, published at Paris in 1888, and which contains the Arab text of the story of Aladdin, along with an exhaustive notice of certain manuscripts of the ' Thousand and One Nights,' and of Galland's translation.

The fourth and fifth volumes of Burton's ' Supplemental Nights ' contain certain new stories from an Arabic manuscript of the ' Nights ' in seven volumes, brought to Europe by Edward Wortley Montague, Esq., and bought at the sale of his library by Dr. Joseph White, Professor of Hebrew and Arabic at Oxford, from whom it passed into the hands of Dr. Jonathan Scott, who sold it to the Bodleian Library, at Oxford, for fifty pounds.

Wortley Montague's manuscript contains many additional tales not included in the Calcutta, Boulak, or Breslau editions, and these additional stories Burton has now translated. It is uncertain how or where Wortley Montague obtained his copy of the ' Thousand and One Nights.' Dr. White had at one time intended to translate the whole lot, but this was never accomplished. Jonathan Scott did, however, translate some of the stories, which were published in the sixth volume of his 'Arabian Nights Entertainment' in A.D. 1811, but the work was badly and incompletely done. It has now been thoroughly revised and put into better form by Burton in these two volumes.

In Appendix I. to Volume V. there is a catalogue of the contents of the Wortley Montague MS., which is very interesting, as it contains not only a description of the manuscript itself, but also a complete list of the tales making up the 'Thousand and One Nights,' many of which are, of course, to be found in the 'Nights' proper.

These two supplemental volumes contain 25 principal and 31 subordinate stories, or 56 in all. Some of them are very amusing, especially the tales of the Larrikins, while the whole add to our knowledge of this vast répertoire of tales from the East, which has been gradually brought to the notice of Europe during the last one hundred and eighty-five years.

Burton's sixth supplemental volume contains certain stories taken from a book of Arabian tales, a continuation of the 'Arabian Nights Entertainment,' brought out by Dom Chavis, a Syrian priest, and eventually teacher of Arabic at the University of Paris, and Mr. Jacques Cazotte, a well-known French *littérateur*, unfortunately and unjustly guillotined in Paris on the 25th September, 1792, at the time of the Revolution.

This work, sometimes called 'The New Arabian Nights,' is an imitation of Galland's marvellous production, and may be considered a sort of continuation of it. Dom Chavis brought the manuscripts to France, and agreed with Mr. Cazotte to collaborate, the former translating the Arabic into French, and the latter metamorphosing the manner and matter to the style and taste of the day. The work first appeared in 1788-89, and was translated into English in 1792.

Burton, in his Foreword to this volume, gives a full account of these stories, as translated and edited by Chavis and Cazotte. He himself gives a translation of eight of them, one of which, The Linguist, the Duenna, and the King's Son, is interesting, as it contains a series of conundrums, questions and answers, which may remind the reader of the story of Abu Al-Husn and his slave-girl Tawaddud, in the 'Nights' proper, and of the history of Al-Hajjaj bin Yusuf and the young Sayyid, from the Wortley Montague MS. In addition to the eight translated stories, the sixth volume contains a great deal of matter in the shape of appendices, such as—Notes on Zotenberg's work on Aladdin and on various manuscripts of the 'Nights'; Biography of the work and its Reviewers Reviewed; Opinions of the Press, etc.: but though well worthy of perusal by the curious, space does not allow of further allusions to them here.

To sum up, then, shortly, Payne's thirteen volumes contain 193 principal, and 159 subordinate stories, or 352 in all, while Burton's sixteen volumes contain 231 principal, and 195 subordinate stories, or 426 altogether. These numerous stories, translated from the Calcutta (1814-18), Calcutta Macnaghten (1839-42), Boulak (Cairo, 1835-36), Breslau (Tunis), Wortley Montague, Galland and Chavis texts may be considered to form what is commonly called 'The Arabian Nights Entertainment.' They date from A.D. 750, which may be considered as the year of their commencement and that of the Abbaside dynasty, and go on, continually added to, up to A.D. 1600, or even later. Many authors have had a hand in the work, the stories themselves having been derived from Indian, Persian, Arabian, Egyptian, Syrian and Grecian sources, and adapted, more or less, for Arab readers and hearers. And as the manuscripts in some of these stories in different countries do not in any way tally, it must be supposed that no such work as an original copy of the 'Thousand and One Nights' has ever been in existence. The répertoire, consisting of a few stories at first, has gradually grown to such a size that now it may almost be considered to contain the largest and best collection of stories that the world has, as yet, seen.

Mention has been already made in a previous

page of the 'Kathá Sarit Ságara,' or Ocean of the Streams of Story, and a brief description of this work was given in the third chapter of 'Early Ideas' (A.D. 1881). Since then a complete translation of the 'Kathá' has been made by Professor C. H. Tawney, of the Calcutta College, and it has been published in fourteen fasciculi, in the 'Bibliotheca Indica,' by the Asiatic Society of Bengal, 1880-1887. It is to be regretted, for the sake of the student and the anthropologist, that the translation is presented in an expurgated form. Still, the Professor has done his work (and a long and tedious work it must have been) excessively well, while many of his notes, corrigenda and addenda are most interesting.

The 'Arabian Nights' and the 'Kathá Sarit Ságara' occupy respectively the same position in Arabic and Hindoo literature. They are both collections of tales adapted to the people of the country for which they have been written. A perusal of both the works will show how much they differ. The characters and ideas of the heroes and heroines, their thoughts, reflections, speeches, surroundings, and situations are worth studying in the two books as an exposition of the manners and customs, ideas and habits of two distinct peoples. The Hindoo characters, as depicted in their storybook, will be found to be duller, heavier, more reverential, and more superstitious than the characters in the 'Nights.' There are two things, however, common to the two books: the power of destiny, and the power of love, against which it is apparently useless to struggle.

While there are 426 stories in Burton's 'Nights,' there are 330 tales of sorts in Tawney's 'Kathá.' Both works are rather formidable as regards size and quantity of matter; still, after a start has been fairly made, the interest goes on increasing in a wonderful way, until at last one becomes absorbed and interested to a degree that can scarcely be imagined.

The stories in the 'Kathá Sarit Ságara' are supposed to have been originally composed by one Gunádhya, in the Paisacha language, and made known in Sanscrit under the title of 'Vrihat Kathá,' or Great Tale. From this work one Bhatta Somadeva, in the eleventh century A.D., prepared the work now known as the 'Kathá Sarit Ságara,' but probably stories have been added to it since. At present it consists of eighteen books, divided into one hundred and twenty-four chapters, and containing three hundred and thirty stories, along with other matter. Of Gunádhya, the supposed original author, not much is known, but Vatsyayana, in his 'Kama Sutra' (printed privately for the Kama Shastra Society) mentions the name of Gunádhya as a writer whose works he had consulted, and gives frequent quotations from them in his chapter on the duties of a wife. The exact date of Vatsyayana's life is also uncertain; some time not earlier than the first century B.C., and not later than the sixth century A.D., is considered to be the approximate period of his existence.

Like the 'Arabian Nights,' it is highly probable that the 'Kathá' grew by degrees to its present size. Gunádhya's original work is apparently not now extant. Between the time it was written and the time that Somadeva produced his edition of it, many stories may have been added, and the same process may have continued afterwards. Somadeva, however, says: 'I compose this collection, which contains the pith of the "Vrihat Kathá."' Again he writes: 'This book is precisely on the model of that from which it is taken; there is not the slightest deviation; only such language is selected as tends to abridge the prolixity of the work; the observance of propriety and natural connection, and the joining together of the portions of the poem so as not to interfere with the spirit of the stories, are as far as possible kept in view. I have not made this attempt through desire of a reputation for ingenuity, but in order to facilitate the recollection of a multitude of various tales.'

The 'Kathá Sarit Ságara' contains many stories now existing in the 'Pancha Tantra,' or Five Chapters, in the 'Hitopodesa,' or Friendly Advice, in the 'Baital Pachesi,' or Twenty-five Stories of a Demon, and other Indian story-books. Owing to the total absence of dates it is difficult to determine from what sources all these stories were collected. But as some of the same fables and animal stories are to be found in the 'Buddhist Birth Stories,' or Játaka Tales, in the 'Arabian Nights,' and in the 'Kathá,' it may fairly be conjectured that stories of this nature were in early years in considerable circulation, and used as a means of conveying wisdom and advice both to the classes and to the masses in those pre-historic times.

To return to Arab story-books. Mention must be made of 'Antar,' a Bedouin romance, which has been partially translated from the Arabic into English by Terrick Hamilton, Secretary to the British Embassy at Constantinople, and published in London (1820). Mr. Clouston, in his 'Arabian Poetry for English Readers,' Glasgow, 1881, has given an abstract of the story, with some specimens of translations from the original.

The work itself is generally supposed to have been written by Al-Asmai, the philologist and grammarian (born A.D. 740, died A.D. 831), who flourished at the court of Harun-ar-Rashid, and was a great celebrity in his time. It is probable that many of the stories told about Antar and his wonderful deeds came down orally and traditionally to Al-Asmai, who embellished them with his own imagination, aided by a wonderful knowledge of the language and idioms used by the Arabs in their desert wilds.

Antar is the hero, and Abla the heroine, of the romance. Antar himself is supposed to have lived during the sixth century A.D., and to have been the author of one of the seven famous poems suspended at Mecca, and known as the Mua'llakat. Besides this he was distinguished as a great warrior, whose deeds of daring were quite marvellous. The translator had intended to divide the work into three parts. The first ends with the marriage of Antar and Abla, to attain which many difficulties had to be overcome. The second part includes the period when Antar suspends his poem at Mecca, also a work of considerable difficulty. The third part gives the hero's travels, conquests, and death. Mr. Hamilton only translated and published the first part of the three, and the two others have not yet been done into English.

The romance of Antar, though tedious, is interesting, as it gives full details of the life of the Arabs before Muhammad's time, and even after, for the Arab life of to-day is apparently much the same as it was three thousand years ago. It appears to be an existence made up of continual wanderings, constant feud and faction, and perpetual struggles for food, independence and plunder. But in the deserts on the frontiers of Syria, Palestine, Mesopotamia and Baghdad, it is said that the various tribes are now kept much more in subjection by the Turks, owing to the introduction of the breech-loader, against which the Arab and his matchlock and his peculiar mode of warfare is somewhat powerless.

While the 'Arabian Nights' are supposed to treat more of the inhabitants of the towns, the romance of Antar deals more with the inhabitants of the desert. To the student of the Arabic language both works are interesting, as they occupy a prominent and standard place in Arabian literature, and afford much information about the manners and customs, ideas and peculiarities of an ancient and interesting race of people. It must be admitted that both Antar and the 'Arabian Nights' are so long that they rather try the patience of readers not particularly interested in them. Nowadays in England the daily press supplies such a mass of information of all sorts in connection with every branch of society, that a constant and persistent reader of our daily and weekly newspapers can find in them quite an 'Arabian Nights Entertainment' without going further afield. Indeed, the stories concerning the cures effected by certain patent medicines are as wonderful as anything one ever reads in the 'Nights' themselves.

And in addition to the realities and actualities of life, as daily told in our newspapers and law reports, many of which do certainly prove that fact is stranger than fiction, there are numerous writers who keep the public supplied with tales and stories of every kind and description. And from the great demand for such productions, whether issued as the penny dreadful, the thrilling story, or the regulation romance in three volumes, one conclusion can only be drawn, which is—that the human mind, everywhere in the East, West, North and South, is always anxious to be fed or amused with something startling or romantic, dreadful or improbable, exciting or depressing.

It is to be presumed, then, that the 'Nights' filled the vacuum in the minds of the people of that day in the East, much the same as the books and newspapers of our time satisfy the cravings of the humanities of the West, who still seem to be ever in search of something new, even if not true ; something original, even if not trustworthy. Human nature appears to be much the same in all ages and at all times, and the scandals connected with high persons, the memoirs and reminiscences of celebrated ones, and the good sayings of witty ones, have always found much favour with the public generally, whether told as stories, published as books, or printed in the papers. Arabic literature abounds with biographical details and stories about celebrated and distinguished men. It was always the custom and fashion to fill their works with much information of the kind. The same fashion appears to exist in England at the present time, with this advantage, however, that we now get all the details and stories direct from the heroes themselves, and during their lifetime.

CHAPTER V.

ANECDOTES AND ANA.

IN Persian literature there are three celebrated works (Sa'di's 'Gulistan,' or Rose Garden, A.D. 1258; Jawini's 'Negaristan,' or Portrait Gallery, A.D. 1334; and Jami's 'Beharistan,' or Abode of Spring, A.D. 1487, all translated by the Kama Shastra Society), containing an entertaining collection of stories, verses, and moral maxims. In Arabic literature there are many books of the same sort, and in this chapter it is proposed to give a few specimens of stories and philosophic reflections culled from various authors. This will perhaps be more interesting than a lengthened analysis of the works themselves.

The following anecdotes have been taken from the 'Naphut-ul-Yaman' (Breeze or Breath of Yaman), a collection of stories and poetical extracts of various Arabic authors, edited by Ahmad-ash-Shirwani.

1.

Al-Jahiz said: 'I never was put so much to shame as when a woman met me on the road and said, " I have some business with you," and I followed her till we reached the shop of a goldsmith, when she said, " Like this man," and walked away. I stood amazed, and asked the goldsmith to explain the matter. He replied : " This woman wanted me to make her a figure of Satan, and I told her that I did not know his physiognomy ; whereon she brought you !" '

II.

A voracious man paid a visit to a hermit, who brought him four loaves, and then went to fetch a dish of beans ; but when he had come with it, he found that his guest had consumed the bread. Accordingly he departed to bring some more bread, but when he returned with it he saw that the man had devoured the beans. This proceeding was repeated ten times, whereon the host asked his guest to what place he was travelling. He replied, ' To Rei.' ' Wherefore ?' ' I heard of a celebrated physician in that town, and I mean to consult him about my stomach, because I have but little appetite for eating.' ' I have a request to make of you.' ' What is it ?' ' When you return, after having recovered your appetite, please do not pay me a visit again.'

III.

One day the poet Abu Nuwas made his appearance at the gate of the palace of Rashid, who, as soon as he was informed of this, called for eggs, and said to his courtiers : ' Here is Abu Nuwas at the door. Now let each of you take an egg and place it under his body, and when he enters I shall feign to be angry with all of you, and shall exclaim : " Now lay eggs each of you, and if you do not I shall order you all to be beheaded," and we shall see how he will behave.' Then the poet was admitted, and the conversation continued. After a while, however, the Khalif became angry, and manifested his displeasure by exclaiming : ' You are all like hens, and meddle with things that do concern you ; now lay eggs each of you, for that is your nature, or I shall order your heads to be struck off.' Then he looked at the courtier on his right, saying : ' You are the first ; now lay an egg.' Accordingly he made great efforts, and contorting his features, at last drew forth an egg. Then the Khalif addressed the others successively in the same manner, and when the turn of Abu Nuwas came, he struck his sides with his hands, and crowing like a cock, said : ' My lord, hens are useless without a cock. These are hens, and I am their cock.' Hereon the Khalif burst out laughing, and approved of his excuse.

IV.

A certain king was much addicted to women, and one of his viziers warned him of the danger. Shortly afterwards some of his concubines observed that his behaviour towards them had changed, and one of them said: 'My lord, what is this?' He replied: 'One of my viziers (mentioning his name) advised me not to love you.' 'Then,' said the girl, 'present me to him, O king, and do not reveal what I shall do to him.' Accordingly he gave the girl away, and when the vizier was alone with her, she made herself so amiable that he fell in love with her, but she refused to grant him any favour except on condition of allowing her first to ride on his back. He agreed. Accordingly she bridled and saddled him, but meanwhile sent word to the king what was taking place; and when he arrived he saw the vizier in the position alluded to, and said: 'You warned me of the love of woman, and this is the state I see you in.' The vizier replied: 'O king! this is just what I warned you of?'

V.

Once a lion, a fox, and a wolf were associates in the chase, and after they had killed an ass, a gazelle, and a hare, the lion said to the wolf: 'Divide the prey among us;' whereon the latter said: 'The ass will be yours, the hare the fox's, and the gazelle mine;' and the lion knocked his eye out. Then the fox said: 'A curse on him, what a silly division he proposed!' Accordingly the lion said: 'Then do you make the division, O possessor of the brush!' And the fox said: 'The ass will be for your dinner, the gazelle for your supper, and the hare for your luncheon.' The lion said: 'You rogue! who taught you to make such a just distribution?' and Reynard answered, 'The eye of the wolf.'

VI.

A certain king asked his vizier whether habit can vanquish nature, or nature habit? The vizier replied: 'Nature is stronger, because it is a root, and habit a branch, and every branch returns to its root.' Now the king called for wine, and a number of cats made their appearance with candles in their paws, and stood around him; then he said to the vizier: 'Do you perceive your mistake in saying that nature is stronger than habit?' The vizier replied: 'Give me time till this evening.' The king continued: 'You shall have it.' Accordingly the vizier appeared in the evening with a mouse in his sleeve, and when the cats were standing with their candles, he allowed it to slip out, whereon all the cats threw down the candles and ran after it, so that the house was nearly set on fire. Then the vizier said: 'Behold, O king, how nature overcomes habit, and how the branch returns to the root.'

The 'Merzubán námah,' translated from the Persian into Arabic, is said to be of very ancient origin, and to embody good maxims in fables. It was composed, or is supposed to have been composed, by one of the old princes of Persia called Merzuban, a brother of the King Nausherwan the Just, who died A.D. 578. On referring to the great encyclopædical and bibliographical dictionary, edited by Fluegel, it will be found, under No. 11,783, that Haji Khalfa mentions this book, giving, however, its title only, without mentioning the time of its composition, nor the author of it, nor the language in which it had been written. The following are some extracts from this work, and the stories resemble others that have come from the Farther East.

I.

The philosopher Merzubán said : ' I am informed that in a certain district of Aderbaijan there is a mountain as high as the sky, with fine brooks, trees, fruits and herbs. Under the shelter of one of the most beautiful trees a pair of partridges lived most happily, but in the vicinity there was likewise a powerful eagle with his brood, who periodically visited the abode of the partridges and devoured their young ones. When the pair had thus several times lost their progeny, the male proposed that it would either be necessary for them to emigrate to some other locality, or to try some expedient by which they might escape from the rapacity of the eagle. He was of opinion that even in case of failure they might gain some valuable experience that would be of use in future attempts to elude the persecution, and said: "We must at all events make a trial, and may learn something from it, like the donkey who endeavoured to become the companion of the camel." The she-partridge asked, "How was that?" and the male continued:

II.

' " Once a donkey tried to keep up walking with a big camel, who paced lustily, and took long steps, but the ass, being in a hurry, stumbled every moment, and found that he had undertaken an impossible task. He asked the camel, ' How is it I wound my hoofs on the rocks so often, although I constantly look where I am stepping; whilst you, who apparently walk with leisure, never cast a glance at any of the obstacles you meet with, and never hurt yourself?' The camel replied: ' The reason is just because you are short-sighted and of weak intellect; you can look no further than your nose, and are, therefore, disappointed; whereas I look always forward, know the obstacles I am likely to encounter, scan the road to a great distance, and avoid the difficulties, selecting the easiest parts of the way.'" The wise hen said: "To be forewarned is to be forearmed, and this principle I follow." "I have narrated this story to show you that we must look forward, now that the time of laying eggs is at hand, because when our little ones are hatched it may again be too late to try and save them."

'The female partridge said: "This is all very well, but we might fare like the hungry fox who would have lost his life if the ichneumon had not interceded for him with the camel." The male said "How was that?" and the female continued:

III.

'"It is related that a certain fox had a fine large den, in which he collected provisions for the winter and for the summer, fared sumptuously, and never suffered from want. Once, however, a large army of ants invaded his domicile, and made short work of all the victuals he had carefully stored. This misfortune befel him just at a time when the weather happened to be very cold and food scarce, so that he began to feel the pangs of hunger. One morning, however, when he was about to sally forth from his den, he perceived, to his no small astonishment, at the mouth of it a camel kneeling, with the hinder part of his body turned towards him. The fox said to himself, 'Here is good luck,' and made a foolhardy attempt to drag the animal into the cave by tying a rope to its tail, and to commence pulling at it with all his might. To make sure of his prey the fox had tied the other end of the rope to his own body, but when he began to jerk it rather strongly the camel became vexed, jumped up suddenly, and first discharging both urine and dung upon Reynard, began to shake himself violently. The fox dangled in the air, and was repeatedly knocked against the flanks of the gigantic animal. Then the fox repented of his silly attempt to feast on camel meat, and knew that his death-knell would shortly sound. Luckily an ichneumon happened to be standing close by, amazed at the strange spectacle, and the fox implored it to intercede for him. Accordingly, the ichneumon addressed the camel in the following strain: ' Friend giant! it is meet that the strong, hoping for an eternal reward, should have mercy upon the weak! Here is a poor stranger who has accidentally become entangled with your tail. He will be strangled; you may save his life and become his deliverer by letting him go.' The camel then released the fox, who would assuredly have lost his life if the ichneumon had not interceded for him." When the male partridge had heard this story he fully approved of the moral of it, which is to the effect that ignorant and weak individuals are generally foiled in their designs against those who are powerful. He therefore considered that it would be best to throw themselves upon the mercy of the eagle, and said: "We must pay a visit to his majesty the eagle, explain our case to him, implore his mercy, and enroll ourselves among the number of his servants. We may succeed by gaining his favour; he is the king of all the birds, and carnivorous, but for all we know his disposition may be so merciful that he will spare our offspring not only himself, but order all the other birds of prey, his subjects, to do likewise."

'Then the she-partridge exclaimed: "Your advice is indeed wonderful! You propose nothing less than that we should court our own perdition, and of our own accord run into a trap! The eagle in treacherous, and would deal with us like the heron dealt with the little fish." The male said, "Please narrate the occurrence," and the female continued:

IV.

'" A heron had taken up his abode, and had lived for a long time near a brook on the little fishes there. At last, however, he became so old and weak that he was scarcely able to provide his daily food. He was once standing in a melancholy attitude on the bank of the streamlet, waiting for a chance to satisfy his hunger, when he happened to catch sight of a beautiful little fish disporting itself in the water, and mourned over his inability to get hold of it. The little fish perceived the heron standing immovable, and apparently taking not the least notice of it; therefore it gradually ventured to approach him, and asked the cause of his melancholy. The heron replied, 'I am reflecting upon the time of my youth which has passed away, the life I enjoyed, the pleasures I felt, all of which are irretrievably lost, and have left behind nothing but repentance for my sins, a weak body, and tottering limbs. I can now only regret the depredations I have committed, and wash away with my tears the stains of my transgressions. How often have I given occasion, both to little fishes and to eels, to deplore the loss of members of their families, which I had greedily devoured ; but I have now repented, and shall henceforth do so no more.' When the little fish had heard this wonderful confession it asked : ' What can I do for you ?' The heron replied : ' I want you only to convey this declaration of mine, with my salutations, to all your acquaintances, with the information that they may henceforth live in perfect safety, and need not apprehend any depredations on my part. There must, however, be covenants and pledges of security between us.' The little fish asked : ' How can I trust you, since I am the food on which you subsist, and you cannot be inclined to dispense with that.' He said : ' Take this grass and tie it round my neck for a sign that I shall not injure you.' Accordingly, the little fish took hold of a blade of grass, which was to serve for the heron's collar, who then placed his beak near the surface of the water to receive it, but as soon as the little fish had come within reach, the heron gobbled it up, and this was the end of the promised pledge. My dear husband, I have narrated this occurrence only to show that we would, by trusting to any promises of magnanimity that the eagle might make to us, only court our own perdition."

'In spite of all her objections, however, the she-partridge agreed at last to accompany her husband to the court of the eagle. They started together, travelled for some time, arrived at his abode, and made their obeisance to a courtier whose name was Yuyu, whom the male partridge addressed as follows : " Most noble lord, we are denizens of an adjoining mountain, where we lived happily till his majesty the eagle crushed all our hopes by making his appearance on our mountain with his court of birds of prey, destroyed our young on several successive occasions, and reduced us to despair. I proposed to my wife to emigrate, and she at last consented, so that we have now arrived here and placed ourselves under the wings of your protection.' Yuyu was pleased with these words, and replied : " I bid you welcome, and approve of your sagacity which induced you to seek a refuge at the court of our most noble sovereign. I must, however, tell you that although his disposition is righteous, he feeds upon the meat of animals, but when the weak and helpless crave his mercy, or implore his aid, he seldom disappoints them ; those, on the contrary, who oppose or endeavour to deceive him must be prepared to fall under his wrath. He is honest and veracious, because he lives in solitude, and keeps aloof from intercourse with mankind, because all agree that the society of men crushes out all good qualities, and is productive of misery. You may now arise, and seek an audience from his majesty, because the opportunity will not present itself often. When you enter and make your obeisance you must watch his humour, which will be excellent if he has been successful in the chase. Then you will behold him social and chatting with his courtiers, whilst the nightingale, the heron, and other birds are singing and dancing for his amusement, and you can then introduce the subject of your petition. But if you behold him sitting dumb, with bloodshot eyes, or in an angry mood, say nothing if you value your life, and in any case, if you should perceive that silence is best, do not venture to speak."

'After this advice the partridge flew with Yuyu up to a lofty peak of the mountain, and alighted in a beautiful garden, fragrant with the perfume of flowers, where the eagle was sitting with his court, which consisted of birds of every species. Then Yuyu presented himself before his majesty, and craved an audience for the partridge, which, having been granted, he was admitted and spoke as follows: " Praise be to Allah, who has healed our wound and restored us to life ! We lived in trouble and distress, but the justice of your majesty's government is the theme of every tongue ; all our apprehensions have vanished, and we hope for security under the wings of your protection, because it is said that a noble Sultan is to his subjects like a kind father to his children, and protects them against all evils."

'The king replied : " You are welcome in this region ; here you may live in safety among the best of neighbours, and I grant you protection." Accordingly, the partridge returned to his spouse, whom he informed of the condescension of his majesty, whose service both accordingly entered, and whose favour they afterwards gained, so that they lived happily to the end of their days.'

The 'Merzubán námah' contains also several stories about Kesra Nausherwan the Just, and his minister Buzarjimehr, but they are not very interesting. The extracts given above sufficiently show the nature of this work, which puts into the mouths of animals how men and women ought to act under various circumstances, and it bears a strong resemblance in many ways to the 'Kalilah wa Dimnah.'

Two stories have been selected from the celebrated Arabic work entitled 'Al - Mustatraf,' or 'The Gleaner,' or 'The Collector.' The full title of this work is 'Al-Mustatraf min kell finn al-mustazraf,' which may be translated thus : 'Gleanings from every kind of Elegant (or Pleasing) Composition.' The similarity of the first and last word of the title is attributable to the fondness of the Arabs for alliterative or rhyming titles. As there are several meanings attached to the word Mustatraf in the dictionaries, it might also be interpreted as 'The Book of Pleasing Novelties.' It contains an anthology of anecdotes, stories, proverbs, and elegant extracts by Shaikh Muhammad Bin Ahmad Al-Bashihi. The work is mentioned by Fluegel in his edition of Haji Khalfa's great work.

I.

Abbas, the chief of the police of the Khalif Mamun, said: 'One day I was present in an assembly of the Prince of the Faithful, before whom a man was standing heavily fettered with chains of iron. As soon as the Khalif perceived me he said: "Abbas, take good care of this man, and produce him again to-morrow." Accordingly I called for some of my people, and they carried him away, because he was so heavily shackled that he could scarcely move. Considering that I had been ordered to take every care of this prisoner, I concluded that I had better keep him in my own house, in a chamber of which I then confined him. I asked him what place he had come from, and on his replying that it was Damascus, I expressed my best wishes for the prosperity of that town, whereat he was astonished. I told him that I had been there, and asked him about a certain man; he said that he would like to know how I could be acquainted with him, and on my replying that I had had some business with him, he promised to satisfy my curiosity if I gave him first some information. Accordingly I made the following statement:

'"When I was with some other officials at Damascus the population rebelled against us, and even the governor was under the necessity of escaping by getting himself let down in a basket from his palace. I also fled, and whilst doing so the mob pursued me, and I ran into the house of the above-mentioned man, who was sitting at the door of it. I said to him: 'Help me and Allah will help you!' He received me kindly, and told his wife to put me into a certain room, whilst he remained sitting at the door. I had scarcely gone in when my pursuers likewise rushed in and insisted on searching the house, which they actually did, and would certainly have discovered me had not the man's wife kept them off from the room in which I sat trembling for my life. When the people at last dispersed, the man and his wife comforted me as much as they could, and hospitably entertained me in their house for four months, till every danger had passed away. When I was bold enough to go out and see what had become of my slaves, I found that they had all dispersed, and I asked my kind host to allow me to depart to Baghdad. He consented, but when the caravan was starting he insisted on presenting me with a horse, a slave, and all the provisions required for the journey. All these were surprises thrust upon me when I was about to start, and was wondering how I could possibly travel without any of these things. Moreover, during my whole sojourn this kind man had never asked me my name for fear that I might thereby be compromised. After I had safely arrived in Baghdad I desired many a time to show my gratitude to this man, but could obtain no information about him. I still desire to requite his services, and this is the reason why I was so anxious to learn something about him from you."

'After the man had listened to the above statement he said: "Verily, Allah has enabled you to requite the kindness of that man." I asked: "How can that be?" and he replied: "I am that man, but the trouble in which you see me has hindered you from recognising me." Then he reminded me of various circumstances, and so established his identity that I was perfectly convinced of it, and could not restrain myself from embracing him most fervently. To my inquiries how he had fallen into the calamity which had overtaken him, he replied:

'"A disturbance arose in Damascus similar to the rebellion which had broken out when you were there: the Prince of the Believers sent troops and suppressed it, but I, having been suspected as one of the ringleaders thereof, was captured by his command, brought as a prisoner to Baghdad, and considered to have forfeited my life, which I shall certainly lose. I left my family without taking leave, but a slave of mine has followed me here, and will carry back information about me. He is to be found at such and such a place, and if you will send for him I will give him the necessary instructions. I shall consider it a high favour, and as a reward for all the obligations under which you were to me."

'I told him to put his trust in Allah, and got a smith to relieve him first of his irons, then I made him enter the bath, provided him with good clothes, and sent for his slave, to whom he gave, with tears in his eyes, the message for his family. I then ordered my people to get ready several horses and mules, which I loaded with baggage and provisions, gave the man a bag of ten thousand dirhems, with another of five thousand dinars, and ordered my lieutenant to escort him on his journey to Damascus as far as Anbar. But the man replied: "The Prince of the Believers considers that I have committed high treason, and will send troops to pursue me; I shall be recaptured and executed, and by allowing me to escape you will endanger your own life." I said: "Never mind what will became of me, but save your life, and I shall afterwards endeavour to save mine." He rejoined: "That shall not be, and I cannot leave Baghdad without knowing what has become of you. Seeing him determined in his purpose, I ordered my lieutenant to take him to a certain place in the town where he could remain in concealment till the next day, when he might be informed as to whether I had extricated myself from the difficulty, or had lost my life, in which latter case I should only have repaid him for having risked his in Damascus to save mine, and after that he could depart.

'The lieutenant had taken the man away, and I made preparations for my death, getting ready my winding-sheet in which my corpse was to be shrouded, when an official on the part of Mamun arrived with this message: "The Prince of the Faithful orders you to bring the man with you." Accordingly I hastened to the palace, where I found the Khalif sitting and expecting me. The first words he said to me were these: "I want to see the man!" I remained silent, and on his uttering them more emphatically, replied: "Will you please listen to me, O Commander of the Believers?" He continued: "I am determined to strike your head off if the man has fled." I said: "O Prince of the Faithful, the man has not escaped, but listen to what I have to say about him, and then you may act as you deem fit." He continued: "Speak!" Accordingly I narrated everything, and said that I was anxious to requite the man in some measure for all the good he had done to me, that I was desirous to save his life even at the cost of my own, if need be, and finished my explanation by showing the winding-sheet I had brought with me. After the Khalif had patiently listened, he exclaimed: "His merit is superior to yours, because he has treated you nobly without knowing you; whereas you only do so after having enjoyed his beneficence. I desire to reward him myself." "The man is here, and would not leave until apprized of my fate; I can produce him at once." The Khalif said: "This trait of his character is yet more noble; go, comfort the man, and bring him here." Accordingly I departed, and when I introduced the man to the Khalif, he received him kindly, offered him a seat, conversed with him till dinner was brought in, of which he made him partake in his own company. Lastly, the Khalif invested him with a robe of honour, and wished to appoint him Governor of Damascus, but this he humbly refused. Accordingly, Mamun presented him with ten horses saddled and bridled, ten mules caparisoned, and ten bags, each of which contained ten thousand dinars; he also gave him ten slaves, with animals to ride upon, and a letter to the Governor of Damascus to absolve him from the payment of taxes. This man afterwards corresponded with Mamun, and when a courier arrived from Damascus the Khalif used to say to me, "Abbas! a letter from your friend has arrived."'

II.

One night Harun-ar-Rashid was quite sleepless, and said to his vizier, Jaafar, the son of Yahya, the Barmekide: 'I cannot sleep this night; I feel oppressed, and do not know what to do.' The servant Masrur, who happened to be standing near, burst out laughing at these words, and the Khalif continued: 'What are you laughing for? Do you mock me or wish to show your levity?' Masrur said: 'I swear by your relationship to the Prince of Apostles that I have done this unwittingly; but last evening I was near the castle, and walked to the bank of the Tigris, where I saw many persons assembled around a man who made them laugh, and just now I recollected some of his words, which caused me to smile; his name is Ben Almugázeli, and I crave pardon from the Commander of the Faithful.' Then Rashid said: 'Bring him here this moment.' Accordingly Masrur went to Ben Almugázeli and said to him: 'The Commander of the Faithful wants you.' He replied: 'To hear is to obey!' And Masrur continued: 'But on the condition that if he presents you with anything, one-fourth of it will belong to you, and the rest to me.' The man rejoined: 'No, I must have one-third of it and you the other two-thirds.' Masrur would not agree to this proposal, but at last consented after a great deal of haggling. When he was admitted and had made his salutations, the Khalif said: 'If you make me laugh I shall give you five hundred dinars, but if not I shall give you three blows with this sock.' Now Ben Almugázeli said to himself:

" What is the odds if I get three strokes with the sock ?" because he thought it was empty. Accordingly he began to jest and to play tricks at which low people might have laughed, but not Rashid, who did not even smile. The man was first astonished, then grieved, and at last frightened when Rashid said : " Now you have deserved the blows." He then took up the sock and twisted it, but at the bottom there were some balls, each of which weighed two drachms. When he had struck Ben Almugázeli once, the latter yelled pitifully, but recollecting the condition Masrur had imposed upon him, he exclaimed : " Mercy, O Commander of the Faithful, listen to two words of mine." He said : " Speak what you like." The man continued : " I have promised Masrur to let him have two-thirds of the bounty I might receive, and to keep one-third for myself, and to this he agreed only after much bargaining. Now the Commander of the Faithful has decided that the bounty shall consist of three blows, of which my share would be one, and Masrur's two. I have received mine, and now is his turn to take his." Rashid laughed, called for Masrur, and struck him ; Masrur groaned from pain, and said : " I present him with the remainder." The Khalif laughed and ordered them to be presented with one thousand dinars, of which each received five hundred, and Ben Almugázeli went away grateful.'

In this work there are several other stories

concerning various Khalifs, the Barmekide family, and other people, but the extracts given above are sufficient to show the nature of the volume.

Two short anecdotes are taken from the 'Sihr-ul-oyoon,' or 'Magic of the eyes,' a work known to Haji Khalfa, and noted by Fluegel in his lexicon. This book contains seven chapters, with some drawings of the eye, and an appendix consisting entirely of poetry, which, however, is also interspersed throughout the work, excepting in the chapters treating on the anatomy, the infirmities of, and the remedies for the eye.

I.

Moghairah bin Shabah states that he never was so cunningly deceived as by a youth of the Benou-ul-Háreth. He intended to sue for the hand of a girl of that tribe, when this youth, who stood near him, said: 'O Amir, you have no need of her.' 'Why?' 'I saw a man kiss her.' Accordingly Moghairah went away, but heard some time afterwards that the said youth had married the girl himself. On meeting again Moghairah said to the youth: 'Did you not tell me that you had seen a man kiss her.' 'Certainly I did,' the young man replied, 'but that man was her father.'

II.

A man happened to find on the road a silver brooch, which women use for applying collyrium to their eyes. This pin was handsome, and he concluded that the girl who had lost it must have very beautiful eyes. He indulged so much in this fancy that he conceived an affection for the owner of the brooch, and was fond of showing the precious article to his acquaintances. One day a friend paid him a visit, and after the wine they had drunk had taken effect, he took out the said brooch according to his wont, kissed it, and wept over it. The friend, who knew the brooch, asked whence he had obtained it, but he replied : 'Pray do not question me, I am in love with the proprietress of it ; my heart is melting, and it is so dear to me that I get jealous when other eyes beside my own look at it.' The friend said : ' I shall bring about a meeting between you and your mistress.' The other asked, ' Who could procure me that felicity ?' The friend went away, but returned in a short time bearing a covered platter, which he placed before him, saying, ' Uncover this basin,' and lo ! it contained a female head, weltering in its own gore, and on beholding it the man nearly fainted with grief. His friend, however, said : ' Be not dismayed, but tell me how you obtained this brooch, which I had presented to my wife, whose head is before you.' He replied that he had found the brooch on a certain day on the road, and described the spot, adding that he imagined the owner of it must be beautiful, and conceived a warm affection for her, but that he had never seen her face, and knew not who she might have been. The friend said: 'This is true enough, because she told me one day that she had lost it; hence no blame rests on you.' The two men parted; the would-be lover, however, took this melancholy event so much to heart that he not only repented of his folly, but died of grief.

The following curious philosophic discourse is taken from the 'Siraj-ul-Mulúk,' or Lamp of Kings, a well-known work composed about A.D. 1126, and typographed at Cairo A.D. 1872:

'Allah, the Most High, has said (Koran, vi., verse 38): "There is no kind of beast on earth, nor fowl which flieth with its wing, but the same is a people like unto you." Allah the Most High has accordingly established a resemblance between us and all the animals. It is well known that they are not like us in their figures and forms as perceived by the eye, but in their demeanour; and there is not a human being who does not possess some qualities peculiar to animals. When you perceive that a man's character is unusual, you must endeavour to find out the qualities of the animal with which it may be compared, and judge of him according to these; and to avoid all misunderstanding, and to maintain intercourse with him, you must behave towards him in conformity with them.

'Accordingly, when you see an ignorant man of rude behaviour, strong in body, whose anger overpowers him at any moment, you are to compare him to a tiger, and there is an Arab proverb: " He is more stupid than a tiger." When you see a tiger, you avoid him, and do not fight with him, therefore towards an individual of this kind you must behave in the same manner.

'When you observe a man wantonly attacking the reputation of others, compare him to a dog, because it is his nature. When a dog barks at you it does not trouble you much, and you go your own way. You must deal in this manner with such men, because they are like dogs who assault others without any provocation.

'When you perceive that a man's nature is to say " Yes " when you say " No," and " No " if you say " Yes," compare him to an ass, because when you approach him he recedes, and when you move away he will move towards you. You must put up with your donkey, and neither separate from him nor insult him. Deal in the same way with such a person.

'When you perceive a man searching out the weaknesses or shortcomings of people, compare him to a fly, which settles on a carcase, and then gluts itself with the vilest parts of it, such as the rotten flesh and the filthy offal.

'When you observe a Sultan taking the lives, and confiscating the property of his subjects, consider him to be a lion, and be on your guard that he does not injure you.

'When you see a wicked man full of tricks and boastings, compare him to a fox.

'If you happen to meet with a tale-bearer who foments enmity among friends, consider him to be a "Zeriban," which is a small beast of fetid smell, so that when two persons fall out with each other, the Arabs say that "a Zeriban has passed between them." It is, indeed, the peculiarity of this animal that an assembly disperses when it enters, accordingly it is driven off as soon as perceived, and a tale-bearer ought to be dealt with similarly.

'When you observe that a man loathes to listen to intelligent conversation, and hates meetings of learned men, but is fond of gossip, all kinds of nonsense, and scandals of society, compare him to the May-bug, which delights in impure exhalations, and loves dunghills, but hates the perfumes of musk or of roses, which actually kill it when sprinkled upon it.

'If you meet an individual displaying a great deal of piety outwardly, but always intriguing to acquire property, to enrich himself by unrighteous means, and to cheat widows and orphans, consider him to be a wolf:

> "The wolf is so devout;
> You see him on his knees,
> He nicely prays and sighs.
> But when his game is near,
> He falls upon it speedily
> And tears it all to pieces."

'When you discover a liar consider him to be

like a dead man, who can give no information, and with whom no one can associate. A liar may also be compared to an ostrich which buries all its eggs in the sand, but leaves one upon the surface, and one close under it, whilst all the others are deeply concealed. When an inexperienced man perceives that egg he takes it, and perhaps also the one close below it, and after scraping up the sand a little, and finding nothing more goes away; whilst a person who knows this habit of the ostrich does not stop searching until he has got possession of all the eggs. You must deal in the same manner with a liar, and not believe him till you get to the bottom of his story, *i.e.* until you elicit the actual truth.

'When you observe that a man's whole attention is absorbed in endeavours to make a good appearance by keeping his clothes nice, and apprehensive lest they should be dirtied in any way, always picking any little straws that might adhere to them, and constantly adjusting his turban, consider him to be a peacock, whose nature is always to admire his own person, to stalk about majestically, to display the plumage of his tail, and to solicit praise of his beauty.

'If you become acquainted with a rancorous person who never forgets the slightest insult, but avenges himself for it even after a considerable lapse of time, compare him to a camel, for the Arabs truly say of such a man that "he is more rancorous than a camel." Avoid such a man as you would an ill-natured camel.

'When you meet a hypocrite, who is different from what he appears to be, compare him to the Yarbu, *i.e.* the mouse of the desert, which has two apertures to its lair, the one for an entrance, and the other for an exit, so that it always cheats the hunter who digs for it.'

Yet another story-book may be quoted, viz., the 'Ilam en Nâs,' or Warnings for Men, containing historical tales and anecdotes of the time of the early Khalifates. Some of these were translated by Mrs. Godfrey Clerk in 1873 (King and Co.), and her little volume also contains a very good genealogical table of the families of the Prophet, and of the Rashidin (or 'rightly directed,' *i.e.* Abu Bakr, Omar, Othman, and Ali), the Omaiyide, and the Abbaside Khalifs.

Among the many works of Arabic literature one of the most interesting and the most amusing is Ibn Khallikan's celebrated Biographical Dictionary. The author must have been a very intelligent and a very industrious man, for his volumes contain an enormous amount of information about many hundred Arabs. This work is rendered all the more readable and all the more amusing by the many anecdotes related in connection with their lives, and a few of these stories are now given below.

I.

Ibn Abbas, son of Abbas, uncle of Muhammad, was one of the ablest interpreters of the Koran. It was owing to his efforts that the study of the poems, composed before the introduction of Islamism, became of such importance to the Muslims, for he frequently quoted verses of the ancient poets in proof of the explanation he gave of different passages of the Koran, and he used to say: 'When you meet with a difficulty in the Koran look for its solution in the poems of the Arabs, for these are the registers of the Arabic nation.' On being asked how he had acquired his extensive knowledge, he replied: 'By means of an inquiring tongue and an intelligent heart.'

It may here perhaps be stated that the Koran, composed avowedly in the purest Arabic, offered many difficulties to those who were not acquainted with the idiom of the desert Arabs, a race who alone spoke the language in its perfection. The study of the ancient poets was therefore considered as necessary for the intelligence of the Koran, and their poems, often obscure from the intricacy of their construction and their obsolete terms, required the assistance of grammatical analysis and philology to render them comprehensible.

II.

Ibn Faris ar-Razi, the Philologist, is the author of these verses:

'Well, some things succeed and some fail: when my heart is filled with cares I say: "One day perhaps they may be dispelled." A cat is my companion; books the friends of my heart; and a lamp my beloved consort.'

III.

Badi Az-Zaman al-Hamadani, the author of some beautiful epistles and excellent essays, which last Hariri took as a model in the composition of his, wrote as follows about death: 'Death is awful till it comes, and then it is found light; its touch seems grating till felt, and then it is smooth; the world is so hostile and its injustice so great that death is the lightest of its inflictions, the least of its wrongs. Look, then, to the right; do you see aught but affliction? Look to the left; do you see aught but woe?

IV.

Abu Wathila Iyas Al-Kadi was renowned for his excessive acuteness of mind, observation, and penetration. Many stories are told about him in connection with these qualities, which are really astonishing. It is related of him that he said: 'I was never worsted in penetration but by one man: I had taken my seat in the court of judgment at Busra, when a person came before me and gave testimony that a certain garden, of which he mentioned the boundaries, belonged to a man whom he named. As I had some doubts of his veracity, I asked him how many trees were in that garden, and he said to me, after a short silence: "How long is it since our lord the Kadi has been giving judgment in this hall?" I told him the time. "How many beams," said he, "are there in the roof?" On which I acknowledged that he was in the right, and I received his testimony.'

V.

It is a curious circumstance that Homer the Greek poet, Radaki the Persian poet, and Bashshar bin Burd the Arabian poet, were all blind. Here is a specimen of one of the verses of the last-named:

'Yes, my friends! my ear is charmed by a person in that tribe; for the ear is sometimes enamoured sooner than the eye. You say that I am led by one whom I never saw; know that the ear as well as the eye can inform the mind of facts.'

He composed also the following verse, which is the most gallant of any made by the poets of that epoch:

'Yes, by Allah! I love the magic of your eyes, and yet I dread the weapons by which so many lovers fell.'

VI.

Several sayings of Al-Hasan bin Sahl, the vizier to the Khalif Al-Mamun, have been preserved. Once he himself wrote at the end of a letter of recommendation, dictated to his secretary: 'I have been told that on the day of judgment a man will be questioned respecting the use he made of the influence given him by his rank in the world, in the same manner as he will be questioned respecting the use he made of the superfluity of his wealth.'

Again he said to his sons: 'My sons, learn the use of language; it is by it that man holds his pre-eminence over other animals; the higher the skill which you attain in the use of language, the nearer you approach to the ideal of human nature.'

VII.

It is related of Sari-as Sakati, the celebrated Sufi, that he said that for twenty years he never ceased imploring Divine pardon for having once exclaimed, 'Praise be to God!' and on being asked the reason he said: 'A fire broke out in Baghdad, and a person came up to me and told me that my shop had escaped, on which I uttered these words; and even to this moment I repent of having said so, because it showed that I wished better to myself than to others.'

VIII.

Al-Ahnaf bin Kais, whose prudence was proverbial among the Arabs, used to say : 'I have followed three rules of conduct, which I now mention merely that the man of reflection may profit by my example—I never interfered between two parties unless invited by them to do so ; I never went to the door of these people (meaning princes) unless sent for by them ; and I never rose from my place to obtain a thing when all men were anxious to possess it.'

IX.

Abu Yazid Taifur al-Bastaimi, the famous ascetic, being asked how he had acquired his knowledge of the spiritual world, answered that it was by means of a hungry belly and naked body. He used to say : 'When you see a man possessing miraculous powers, so as even to mount into the air, let not that deceive you, but see if he observes God's commands and prohibitions, if he keeps within the bounds imposed by religion, and if he performs the duties which it prescribes.'

X.

Abul Aswad ad-Duwali, the inventor of grammar, in intelligence one of the most perfect of men, and in reason one of the most sagacious, was notorious for his avarice, and he used to say : 'If we listened to the demands made by the poor for our money, we should soon be worse off than they.' He said also to his sons : 'Strive not to rival Almighty God in generosity, for He is the most bountiful and the most glorious ; had He pleased He would have given ample wealth to all men, so strive not to be generous lest you die of starvation.' It is also related that Abul Aswad had an attack of the palsy, and that he used to go to the market himself, though scarcely able to draw his legs after him, and yet he was rich, and possessed both male and female slaves. A person who knew this accosted him one day, and said : 'God has dispensed you from the necessity of moving about on your own business, why do you not remain seated at home ?' To which he replied : 'No ; I go in and out, and the eunuch says " He is coming," and the boy says " He is coming," whereas, were I to continue sitting in the house, the sheep would urine upon me without any person's preventing them.'

XI.

It is related that on a dispute between the Sunnites and Shiites of Baghdad about the relative merits of Abu Bakr and Ali, both parties agreed to abide by the opinion of the Shaikh Abul Faraj bin Al-Jauzi. They consequently deputed a person, who questioned him on the subject when he was seated in the preacher's chair. The one reply which

he made bears in Arabic two different meanings—
the first, that the best of them was he whose
daughter was married to the other man; and the
second, that the best of them was he who had
married the daughter of the other man. He then
withdrew promptly, lest he should be questioned
further, and the Sunnites said: 'He means Abu
Bakr, because his daughter Ayesha was married
to the Prophet.' 'Nay,' said the Shiites, 'he
means Ali, because Fatima, the Prophet's daughter,
was married to him.' The answer was certainly
very clever; had it even been the result of long
reflection and deep consideration, it would have been
admirable, but coming as it did without any previous
preparation, it was still more so.

XII.

Shibab Ad-Din (flambeau of the faith) as-Suhra-
wardi was a pious and holy Shaikh, most assiduous
in his spiritual exercises, and the practice of devo-
tion, and successfully guided a great number of
Sufis in their efforts to obtain perfection. Many
persons wrote to him for his opinion on circumstances which concerned themselves, and one wrote
as follows: 'My lord,—If I cease to work I shall
remain in idleness, and if I work I am filled with
self-satisfaction; which is best?' To this the
Shaikh replied: 'Work, and ask Almighty God

to pardon thy self-satisfaction.' The following is one of his verses :

'If I contemplate you, I am all eyes; and if I think of you I am all heart.'

XIII.

Abu Ali Al-Jubbai was an able master in the science of dogmatic theology, and had at one time a pupil named Abul Hasan Al-Ashari. It is related that one day the two had the following discussion. Al-Ashari propounded to his master the case of three brothers, one of whom was a true believer, virtuous and pious; the second an infidel, a debauchee, and a reprobate; and the third an infant; they all died, and Al-Ashari wished to know what had become of them. To this Al-Jubbai answered: 'The virtuous brother holds a high position in Paradise, the infidel is in the depths of hell, and the child is among those who have obtained salvation.' 'Suppose now,' said Al-Ashari, 'that the child should wish to ascend to the place occupied by his virtuous brother, would he be allowed to do so?' 'No,' replied Al-Jubbai, 'it would be said to him : " Thy brother arrived at this place through his numerous works of obedience towards God, and thou hast no such works to set forward."' 'Suppose, then,' said Al-Ashari, 'that the child say, "That is not my fault; you did not let me live long enough, neither did

you give me the means of proving my obedience." '
'In that case,' answered Al-Jubbai, 'the Almighty
would say : " I knew that if I allowed thee to live
thou wouldst have been disobedient, and incurred
the severe punishment of hell ; I therefore acted
for thy advantage."' 'Well,' said Al-Ashari, 'and
suppose the infidel brother were here to say : "O
God of the Universe ! since you knew what
awaited him, you must have known what awaited
me ; why, then, did you act for his advantage and
not for mine?"' Al-Jubbai had not a word to
offer in reply. This discussion proves that the
Almighty elects some for mercy, and others for
punishment, and that his acts are not the results
of any motive whatsoever.

XIV.

It is related that As-Shafi said : 'There are five
men on whom people must rely for the nourish-
ment of their minds : he who wishes to become
learned in jurisprudence must have recourse to Abu
Hanifah ; he who desires to become skilled in
poetry must apply to Zoheir bin Ali Sulma, the
author of one of the Mua'llakas, or suspended
poems at Mecca ; he who would like to become
well acquainted with the history of the Muslim
conquests must obtain his information from
Muhammad bin Ishak ; he who wishes to become
deeply learned in grammar must have recourse to
Al-Kisai ; and he who seeks to be acquainted with

the interpretations of the Koran must apply to Mukatil bin Sulaiman.'

XV.

There are several stories current as to how the Khalif Omar bin Al-Khattab took upon himself the title of 'Commander of the Faithful.' One is that Omar was one day holding a public sitting, when he said: 'By Allah! I do not know what we must say. Abu Bakr was the successor of the Apostle of God, and I am the successor of the successor of God's Apostle. Is there any title that can answer?' Those who were present said: 'Commander (Amir) will do.' 'Nay,' said Omar, 'you are all commanders.' On this Al-Mughira said: 'We are the faithful, and you are our Commander.' 'Then,' said Omar, 'I am the Commander of the Faithful.'

XVI.

Abu Ali Yahya, the vizier of Harun-ar-Rashid, was the son of Khalid, and the grandson of Barmek. Yahya was highly distinguished for wisdom, nobleness of mind, and elegance of language. One of his sayings was: 'Three things indicate the degree of intelligence possessed by him who does them: the bestowing of gifts, the drawing up of letters, and the acting as ambassador.' He used to say to his sons: 'Write down the best things which you hear; learn by heart the best things which you write down; and in speaking utter the best things which you have learned by heart.'

XVII.

Ibn As-Sikkit, the philologist, related that Muhammad bin As-Summak used to say: 'He who knows mankind humours them; he who has not that knowledge thwarts them; and the main point in humouring mankind is to abstain from thwarting them.' The neglect of carrying out this maxim cost As-Sikkit his life. One day, whilst he was with the Khalif Al-Mutwakkil, that prince's two sons, Al-Motazz and Al-Muwaiyad, came in, and the Khalif said to him: 'Tell me, Yakub, which you like best—these two sons of mine, or Al-Hasan and Al-Hussain, the sons of Ali.' Ibn As-Sikkit answered by depreciating the merits of the two princes, and giving to Al-Hasan and Al-Hussain the praise to which they were well entitled. On this Al-Mutwakkil ordered his Turkish guards to chastise him, and they threw him down and trod on his belly. He was then carried to his house, where he died two days afterwards, A.D. 859.

XVIII.

Three men met together; one of them expressed a wish to obtain a thousand pieces of gold, so that he might trade with them; the other wished for an appointment under the Emir of the Muslims;

the third wished to possess the Emir's wife, who was the handsomest of women, and had great political influence. Yusuf bin Tashifin, the Emir of the Muslims, being informed of what they said, sent for the men, bestowed one thousand dinars on him who wished for that sum, gave an appointment to the other, and said to him who wished to possess the lady : ' Foolish man ! what induced you to wish for that which you can never obtain ?' He then sent him to her, and she placed him in a tent, where he remained three days, receiving each day, one and the same kind of food. She had him then brought to her, and said : ' What did you eat these days past ?' He replied : ' Always the same thing.' 'Well,' said she, 'all women are the same thing !' She then ordered some money and a dress to be given him, after which she dismissed him.

The following anecdotes have been gathered from various sources.

I.

A certain shepherd had a dog of which he was very fond, and which having, to his great grief, died, was buried by him with every mark of affection and regret. The Kadi of the village, whose ill-will the shepherd had in some way incurred, hearing of this, ordered him to be brought before him on the serious charge of profanity in having mocked the ceremonies of the

Muhammadan religion, and buried an unclean animal with sacred rites. On being asked what he had to say in his defence, the prisoner thus addressed the magistrate: 'If your reverence will be pleased to hear my story, you will, I am sure, excuse me. My dog's mother died when he was quite a puppy, and he was brought up by a she-goat of my flock, who adopted him. When she died in her turn she left him all her property, consisting of several fine young kids. Now when my dog was taken ill, and found himself at the point of death, I asked him what I should do with the kids which belonged to him, and he replied: "Give them to his reverence the Kadi." I thought the animal so sensible for this that I gave him Muslim burial.' 'Quite right,' said his reverence. 'What else was the lamented deceased pleased to observe?'

II.

A knowledge of the language of birds and beasts is regarded as the greatest divine gift, and was expressly vouchsafed, according to the Koranic legend, to Solomon, the son of David. It is related that one day Solomon was returning to his palace when he saw a cock and hen sparrow sitting near the gateway, and overheard the former telling the latter that he was the person who had designed, and planned, and built all the surroundings. On hearing this Solomon remarked to the male bird that he must know he was telling a fearful lie, and that nobody would believe him. 'That is true,' replied the sparrow, 'nobody probably will believe my story except my wife; she believes implicitly everything that I say.'

III.

One day a king was sailing in a boat with a negro slave, who was so seasick that his groans and lamentations disturbed the royal repose. A doctor who happened to be present undertook to keep the slave quiet, and, on receiving permission to do so, ordered him to be thrown overboard, which was promptly done. The poor wretch managed with difficulty to catch hold of the rudder of the boat, and, being taken on board once more, sat shivering in a corner, and did not utter another sound. The king, delighted with this result, asked the doctor how he had silenced the fellow. 'Your Majesty will see,' was the reply, 'he had never before experienced the inconvenience of being drowned, and did not properly appreciate the security of a boat.'

IV.

One day the Khalif Harun-ar-Rashid and his jester, the poet Abu Nuwas, were disputing as to the truth of an axiom laid down by Abu Nuwas, that 'an excuse was often worse than the crime,' and the poet offered to convince the monarch of it before the night was over. The Khalif, with a grim humour peculiarly his own, promised to take off his jester's head if he failed to do so, and went out in a rage. After awhile Harun came in a somewhat surly temper to his harem, and the first thing which greeted him was a kiss from a rough-bearded face. On calling out violently for a light and an executioner, he found that his assailant was Abu Nuwas himself. 'What on earth, you scoundrel, do you mean by this conduct?' asked the enraged Sovereign. 'I beg your Majesty's most humble pardon,' said Abu Nuwas, 'I thought it was your Majesty's favourite wife.' 'What!' shrieked Harun, 'why the excuse is worse than the crime.' 'Just what I promised to prove to your Majesty,' replied Abu Nuwas, and retired closely followed by one of the imperial slippers.

V.

An Arab whose camel had strayed swore an oath that he would, on finding it, sell it for one dirhem. When he had again obtained possession of the animal he repented of his oath, but tied a cat to the neck of the camel and shouted: 'Who will buy a camel for one dirhem, and a cat for a hundred dirhems? But I will not sell them separately.' A man who was there said: 'How cheap would this camel be if it had no collar on the neck!' Something of the same kind happened in France the other day. A peasant died, leaving his property to be sold by his wife. Among other things there was a dog and a horse, which the woman put up for sale together, saying that the dog's price was twenty pounds, and the horse's one pound, but that they must be sold together. It turned out that the deceased husband had left the dog to his wife, and the horse to another relation, the monies realized by the sale of each to be paid to the respective parties.

VI.

An Arab of the desert said to his boy: 'O son! on the day of resurrection thou wilt be asked what merit thou hast gained, and not from whom thou art descended; that is to say, thou wilt be asked what thy merit is, and not who thy father was.'

VII.

A learned man relates the following: 'I stood with a friend on a road conversing with him when a woman halted opposite to me, looking at me steadfastly. When this staring had passed all bounds, I despatched my slave to ask the woman what she was listening to. He came back and reported that the woman had said: "My eyes had committed a great sin. I intended to inflict a punishment upon them, and could devise none worse than looking at that hideous face." '

There are some good verses in the Arabic descriptive of the places where certain Arabs wished to be buried. It was Abu Mihjan, the Thackifite, who chose the vineyard.

' Bury me, when I die, by the roots of the vine,
The moisture thereof will distil into my bones ;
Bury me not in the open plain, for then I much fear
That no more again shall I taste the flavour of the grape.'

Another version :

' When the Death angel cometh mine eyes to close,
  Dig my grave 'mid the vines on the hill's fair side ;
For though deep in earth may my bones repose,
  The juice of the grape shall their food provide.
Oh, bury me not in a barren land,
  Or Death will appear to me dread and drear !
While fearless I'll wait what he hath in hand
  If the scent of the vineyard my spirit cheer.'

On the other hand, some of the wild people prefer the hill slopes, and an example is given in the address of the dying Bedouin to his tribe :

' O bear with you my bones where the camel bears his load,
  And bury me before you, if buried I must be ;
And let me not be buried 'neath the burden of the vine,
  But high upon the hill whence your sight I ever see !
As you pass along my grave cry aloud, and name your names,
  The crying of your names shall revive the bones of me,
I have fasted through my life with my friends, and in my
    death
  I will feast when we meet on that day of joy and glee.'

The French poet, Alfred de Musset's, gentle verses in his elegy to Lucie, and which have been engraved on his tomb in Paris, at Père-Lachaise, run as follows:

> 'When I shall die, dear friends, aslant
> My silent grave a willow plant;
> I love its foliage weeping near,
> To me its colour's sweet and dear;
> Its shadow gray will lightly fall
> Upon my tomb—a mourning pall,
> And will likewise do the keeping
> Of the ground where I am sleeping.'

APPENDIX.

LIST OF TRANSLATIONS

Published under the patronage of the Old Oriental Translation Fund.

FROM THE PERSIAN.

1. Memoirs of the Emperor Jehanghir.
2. History of the Afghans.
3. The Adventures of Hatim Tai.
4. The Life of Sheikh Muhammad Ali Hazin.
5. Autobiographical Memoirs of the Moghul Emperor Timur.
6. The Life of Hafiz ul Mulk Hafiz Rehmut Khan.
7. The Geographical Works of Sadik Isfahani.
8. Firdusi's Shah Nameh.
9. Private Memoirs of the Moghul Emperor Humayun.
10. History of the Mahomedan Power in India during the Last Century.
11. Customs and Manners of the Women of Persia.
12. Mirkhond's History of the Early Kings of Persia.
13. The Political and Statistical History of Guzerat.
14. Chronique d'Abou Djafar Muhammad Tabari.
15. Laili and Majnun.
16. Practical Philosophy of the Mahomedan People.
17. Specimens of the Popular Poetry of Persia.
18. History of Hyder Naik, otherwise called Nuwab Hyder Ali.
19. The Dabistan, or School of Manners.

20. History of the Reign of Tipu Sultan.
21. Historical Memoirs of Early Conquerors of Hindustan, and Founders of the Ghaznavide Dynasty.

FROM THE ARABIC.

1. The Travels of Ibn Batuta.
2. Travels of Marcarius, Patriarch of Antioch.
3. The Algebra of Muhammad Ben Musa.
4. History of the First Settlement of the Mahomedans in Malabar.
5. Alfiyya, ou le Quintessence de la Grammaire Arabe.
6. Haji Khalfæ Lexicon Encyclopœdicum et Bibliographicum.
7. The History of the Temple of Jerusalem.
8. Histoire des Sultans Mamelouks de l'Egypte.
9. The History of the Mahomedan Dynasties in Spain.
10. El-Mas'udi's Historical Encyclopædia, entitled 'Meadows of Gold and Mines of Gems.'
11. Ibn Khallikan's Biographical Dictionary.
12. Makamat, or Rhetorical Anecdotes of Abul Kasem al Hariri of Basra.
13. The Chronology of Ancient Nations, by Albiruni.

FROM THE SANSCRIT.

1. Kalidasæ Raghuvansa Carmen.
2. Harivansa, ou Histoire de Famille de Harl.
3. The Sánkhya Káriká, or Memorial Verses on the Sánkhya Philosophy.
4. Rig Veda Sanhita.
5. Kumara Sambhava.
6. The Vishnu Purana, a System of Hindu Mythology and Tradition.
7. Sama Veda.
8. Kalidasa, the Birth of the War God.

FROM THE CHINESE.

1. Han Koong Tsew, or the Sorrows of Hen—a Tragedy.
2. The Fortunate Union—A Romance.
3. Hoe Lan Ki—A Drama.

APPENDIX.

4. Le Livre des Récompenses et des Peines.
5. Mémoires sur les Contrées occidentales.

FROM THE JAPONAIS-CHINOIS.

1. San Kokf Tsou Ran To Sets ; ou, Apercu général des trois Royaumes.
2. Annales des Empereurs du Japon.

FROM THE TURKISH.

1. History of the War in Bosnia during 1837-38-39.
2. History of the Maritime Wars of the Turks.
3. Annals of the Turkish Empire, A.D. 1591 to 1659.
4. Narratives of Travels in Europe, Asia, and Africa.

FROM THE ARMENIAN.

1. The History of Vartan, and of the Battle of the Armenians.
2. Chronique de Matthieu d'Edesse.

FROM THE CINGALESE.

1. Yakkun Nattannawa and Kolan Nattannawa, two Cingalese poems.

FROM THE COPTIC.

1. The Apostolic Constitutions, or Canons of the Apostles.

FROM THE ETHIOPIC.

1. The Didascalia, or Apostolical Constitutions of the Abyssinian Church.

FROM THE HEBREW.

1. The Chronicles of Rabbi Joseph Ben Joshua Ben Meir.

FROM THE HINDUSTANI.

1. Les Aventures de Kamrup.

FROM THE MALAY.

1. Memoirs of a Malayan Family.

FROM THE MAGHADI.

1. The Kalpa Sutra and Nava Tatva. Two works illustrative of the Jain Religion and Philosophy.

From the Syriac.

1. Spicilegium Syriacum; containing remains of Bardesan, Meliton, Ambrose, and Mara Bar Serapion.

Miscellaneous.

1. Miscellaneous Translations, two volumes, 1831-34.
2. Translations from the Chinese and Armenian.
3. A Description of the Burmese Empire.
4. Essay on the Architecture of the Hindus.
5. Histoire de la Littérature Hindoui et Hindoustani.
6. Biographical Notices of Persian Poets.
7. The Poems of the Huzailis, edited in Arabic.

INDEX.

A.

Aasha (Al.), the poet, 30, 77, 82
Abbas, uncle of Muhammad, 3, 7
Abbasides, the, 7, 12
Abbaside Khalifs, the most celebrated, 12, 96
Abbaside Khalifs, list of, 19
Abd-al-Hamid, the secretary, 95
Abd-allah bin Hilal, the translator, 90
Abd-allah bin Rewaha, the poet, 34
Abd-allah bin Zobeir, the politician, 34
Abd-ar-Rahman I. of Spain, 8
Abd-ar-Rahman II. of Spain, 9
Abd-ar-Rahman III. of Spain, 9, 11, 102
Abdul-Muttalib, grandfather of Muhammad, 120, 121
Abdul Wahab, the reformer, 16
Abode of Wisdom, 106
Abraham, the father of three religions, 144
Abu Awana, the traditionist, 38
Abu Bakr, the Khalifah, 4, 18, 123, 137, 147
Abu Bakr as Sauli, the editor of poems, 77, 83, 84, 101
Abu Hatim es Sejastani, the philologist, editor of poems and author, 76
Abu Nuwas, the poet, 77, 79-82
Abu Obaida, the general, 4
Abu Obaida, the philologist, 60, 61
Abu Othman, the philologist, 62, 76
Abu Sa'ud, the mufti, 112
Abu Sofyan, the politician and Companion, 34, 137

Abu Sulaiman Dawud ez Zahari, the imam, 38
Abu Tammam, the poet, 76, 77
Abu Thaleb, uncle of Muhammad, 121, 125
Abu Zaid, the traditionist, 38
Abu Zaid bin Aus, the editor of poems, 76
Abul Abbas as Saffah, 7, 19
Abul Aina, the philologist, 63
Abul Ala-al-Maari, the philologist and poet, 84
Abul Atahya, the poet, 77, 78
Abul Faraj, the historian, 97
Abul Faraj al Ispahani, 77, 83, 84, 87
Abul Feda, the historian, 97, 108, 109
Abul Khair, or Ahmed bin Mustafa, 55, 113, 115
Abul Mashar (Albumasar), the astronomer, 24, 42
Ahmed-bin-ud Dinveri, the author, 58
Akhfash (Al), the grammarian, 49
Akhtal (Al), the poet, 77, 78, 82
Alchemists, 40
  (Khalid bin Yazid, Jaafar as Sadik, Jaber bin Hayam, each indexed separately.)
Ali bin Abu Thaleb, the Khalifah, 5, 6, 19, 123, 127
Ali bin Ridhwan, the philosopher, 65, 69, 70
Ali bin Yunis, the astronomer, 43
Amina, mother of Muhammad, 121
Amr bin Al-Aasi, the general, 4, 129, 147

INDEX.

Amra-al-Kais (Amriolkais), the poet, 28, 79, 80
Amru, the poet, 29
Analysis of twelve stories from the 'Arabian Nights,' 157-174
Anbari (Al), the grammarian, 49
Anecdotes, eighteen from Ibn Khallikan's Biographical Dictionary, 217-228
Anecdotes from various sources, 228
Animal fables and stories, 153, 156
Ansari (Al), the philologist, 62
'Antar,' a Bedouin romance, 184, 185
Antara, the poet, 28
Arab verses about burial places, 233
Arabia, description of. 1, 2; history of, 2; detached from the Abbasides, 15; semi-independent, 16; Turkish dealings with, 16; Wahhabi movement in, 16; Egyptian dealings with, 17; Wahhabism in, 17; present government of, 17; future prospects of, 18
Arabian learning, 10, 24
'Arabian Nights,' The. Date of their commencement, 152, 153; the oldest part of the work, 153; the oldest tales and stories, 154; the remaining ones, 154; the sources from which they sprang, 152, 180; many authors composed the work, 153-180; compared with the 'Katha Sarit Ságara,' 181; remarks on the 'Nights' and 'Antar,' 186; Galland's translation of, 154, 175, 176; Payne's, 155, and Burton's 155; stories from, 157-174
Arabic language, 23, 24
Arabic literature, decline of, 117, 118; its former position, 117; its present state, 118
Arabic literature, translation of, vii.
Arabic story books, 151, 152, 184, 188, 192, 201, 210, 212, 216
Asmai (Al), the philologist, 60, 61, 62
Asmai (Al), supposed author of 'Antar,' 184
Astronomers, 41
(Fezari (Al), Abul Máshar, Farghani (Al), Battani (Al),

Ali bin Yunis, Es-Zerkel, each indexed separately.)
Ayesha, third wife of Muhammad, 4, 38, 125, 126, 128, 137, 138
Az-zahra, mistress or wife of Abd-ar-Rahman III. of Spain, 12

B.

Badger (Rev. G. P.), on Muhammad, 120
Badger (Rev. G. P.), about the Koran, 140
Badr, battle of, 127
Baghdad, founding of, 12; description of, 96; fall and conquest of, 12
Baital Pachesi, 183
Baladori (Al), the translator and chronicler, 91
Barmekides, The, 12, 98-101
Bashshar bin Burd, the poet, 77, 78
Battani (Al), or Albategnius, the astronomer, 25, 43
Bekri (Al), the traveller and geographer, 49, 50, 52
Benjamin's (Mr.) 'Persia and the Persians,' 6
Beruni (Al), the traveller and geographer, 49, 50, 51
Biblos, or Book, or Bible, 139; the work of many men, 139; its increased interest after visiting Egypt, Palestine and Syria, 139; can be read in various ways, 139; its description by 'Il Secolo,' 140; as a scientific work of little value, 140
Birgeli, or Birkeli, the dogmatist and grammarian, 112
Bohtori (Al), the poet, 76, 77, 84
Boulak (Cairo) text of the 'Nights,' 156, 180
Breslau (Tunis) text of the 'Nights,' 156, 174, 175, 180
Buddha, 119
Buddha compared with Jesus, 142, 143
Buddhism and Christianity, 142
Buddhist birth stories, or Jataka tales, 181
Bujeir bin Zoheir, the poet, 32
Bukhari (Al), the traditionist, 38, 39

INDEX.

Burton (Richard F.), description of his 'Nights' translation in sixteen volumes, 155, 156, 175-180
Busiri (Al)'s poem of the Mantle, 32, note

C.

Calcutta texts of the 'Nights,' 156, 175, 180
Calligraphers, 113
  (Ibn Mukla, Ibn Al Bawwab, Yakut Al Mausili, Ibn Hilal, Hamdallah, Mir Ali, Muhammad Hussain Tabrizi, each indexed separately.)
Casiri, the bibliographer, 11
Caussin de Perceval, 26, 78, 155
Chavis and Cazotte, the translators, 155, 178, 179
Chinese language, 23
Christianity and Buddhism, 142
Clerk (Mrs. Godfrey), 216
Clouston, W. A., 29, 184
Companions of the Prophet, 39
Compilers of encyclopædias and biographies, 55
  (Nadim (An), Ibn Khallikan, Abul Khair, Haji Khalfa, each indexed separately.)
Contents of this work, ix.-xiv.
Cordova, 7, 8, 9, 11
Cromwell and the Bible, 140

D.

Democracy of Islam, 149
Dow, a translator, 154
Duwali (Ad), the grammarian, 45, 46

E.

Early Ideas,' a group of Hindoo stories, 151, 181
Egypt, the Fatimites established in, 13; invasion of, by Jawhar, 13; conquest of, by Saladin, 13; other dynasties in, 13; conquest of, by Selim the First, 14; incorporated with Turkey, 14
English newspapers, 186
English tales and stories, 186
Epistolography, 95
Erpenius, a translator, 26, 97

Essays and discourses by Hariri, 87, 88
Es-Zerkel, or Arzachel, the astronomer, 44, 45

F.

Fadhl bin Yahya, the Barmekide, 99, 100
Farabi (Al), or Alfarabius, the philosopher, 24, 25, 65, 66, 67
Farazdak, the poet, 77, 78
Farghani (Al), or Alfraganius, the astronomer, 24, 25, 42
Farra (Al), the grammarian, 48
Fatimites, The, 13
Fezari (Al), the astronomer, 41
Firuzabadi, the lexicographer, 110
Fluegel, the translator, 115, 193, 202, 210
France, Invasion of, by the Arabs, 7
Freytag, the translator, 27

G.

Gabriel bin Georgios, the physician, 73, 74
Galland, his translation of the fables of Lokman and Bidpay, 26; and of the 'Nights,' 154, 175, 176; his biography, by Burton, 154; his texts, 180
Gauttier, a translator, 155
Gayangos (Pascual de), the translator, 10, 11, 22, 117
Geographers and travellers, 49
  (Muslim Homeir, Mervezi (Al), Ibn Foslan, Ibn Khordabeh, Jeihani, Istakhri (Al), Ibn Haukul, Beruni (Al), Bekri (Al), Idrisi, Ibn Batuta, each indexed separately.)
Georgios bin Bakhtyeshun, the physician, 72, 73, 98
Ghazali (Al), the mystic and philosopher, 65, 70
God of the Arabs, 148
God of the Jews, 148
Golius, 41, 42
Grammarians, The, 45
  (Duwali (Ad), Khalil (Al), Sibawaih, Jahiz (Al), Kisai (Al), Mubarrad (Al), Thalab, Farra (Al), Akhfash (Al), Shaibani (As), Anbari (Al), each indexed separately.)

16

Granada, Kingdom of, established, 9 ; fall of, 9, 112 ; taken by Ferdinand and Isabella, 9 ; Alhambra at, 11, 112
Gunádhya, the Hindoo author, 182, 183

H.

Habicht, a translator, 155, 175
Hajaj bin Yusuf bin Matta, the translator, 90, 98
Haji Khalfa, the bibliographer, 55, 113, 115
Hakim II. of Spain, his education, 103 ; his diwan of poems, 103 ; his library, 104 ; and catalogue of books, 104, 105
Halaku Khan, 13, 107
Hamdallah, the penman, 113
Hamilton (Terrick), the translator of 'Antar,' 184, 185
Hanbal, the imam, 37
Hanifa, the imam, 37
Hanyfs, The, 133
Harath, the poet, 29
Hariri (Al), the author of the 'Makâmat,' 87, 88
Harun-ar-Rashid, the Khalif, 12, 19, 73, 96-100
Hasan bin Ali, the Fatimite, 5
Hasan bin Sehl, the translator, 91
Hasan bin Thabit, the poet, 34
Hazar Afsaneh, or Thousand Stories, 152
Hazim (Al), the traditionist, 38
Herbelot (D'), the translator and Orientalist, 97
Hertlemah, the hostile poetess, 31
Hijrah, or Emigration, 25
Historians, The, 52
(Ibn Ishak, Ibn Hisham, Wackidi (Al), Muhammad bin Saad, Madaini (Al), Tabari, Masudi, Ibn Athir, Bahauddin, Imad-uddin, Kamaluddin, Abul Feda, Ibn Khaldun, Ibn Hajar, Ibn Kesir, Taki-uddin of Fez, Ibn Arabshaw, Makrisi (Al), Sayuti, Makkari (Al), each indexed separately.)
'Hitopodesa,' a Hindoo story-book, 151, 153, 183
Hobeira, the hostile poet, 31

Honein, Battle of, 130
Honein bin Ishak, the physician and translator, 75, 91
Hughes's 'Dictionary of Islam,' 120, 149
Hussain bin Ali, the Fatimite, 5

I.

Ibn Al Arabi, the mystic, 95
Ibn Al Athir, the historian, 54, 55
Ibn Al Bawwab, the penman, 113, 114
Ibn Al Mukaffa, the translator and author, 89, 91-94, 152
Ibn Arabshaw, the historian, 110
Ibn As Sikkit, the editor of poems, 76
Ibn Bajah (Avempace), the philosopher, 24, 25, 65, 70
Ibn Batlan, the physician and philosopher, 70
Ibn Batuta, the geographer and traveller, 108, 109
Ibn Demash, the editor of poems, 76
Ibn Duraid, the philologist and writer on natural history, 64
Ibn Foslan, the geographer and traveller, 49
Ibn Hajar, the historian and biographer, 109
Ibn Haukul, the geographer and traveller, 49, 50
Ibn Hilal, the penman, 113
Ibn Hisham, the historian, 52
Ibn Ishak, the historian, 52
Ibn Kamal Pasha, a writer on law, 112
Ibn Kesir, the historian, 110
Ibn Khaldun, the historian, 108, 109
Ibn Khallikan, the biographer, 55-57, 116, 216 ; eighteen anecdotes from his work, 217-228
Ibn Khordabeh, the geographer, 49, 50
Ibn Kutaiba, the philologist and author, 63
Ibn Malik, the grammarian, 108
Ibn Mukla, the penman, 113, 114
Ibn Rashid (Averroes), the philosopher, 24, 25, 65, 71
Ibn Sina (Avicenna), the physician, 24, 25, 65, 67, 69

INDEX.

Ibn-ul-Marzaban, the editor of poems, 76
Ibn Wahshiyah, the translator, 91
Ibn Yunis, the historian, 44
Ibrahim of Aleppo, a writer on law, 112
Idrisi, the geographer, 49, 50, 52
'Ilam en nas,' a story-book, 216
Imams, The Shiah, 37
Imams, The Sunni, 37, 38
Isa bin Musa, the physician, 75
Islam, The dogmas, precepts, and ordinances of, 148, 149
Istakhri (Al), the geographer and traveller, 49, 50

J.

Jaafar as Sadik, the alchemist, 41
Jaafar bin Yahya, the Barmekide, 99-101
Jaber (Al), or Geber, the astronomer, 24, 25, 41
Jaber bin Hayam, the alchemist, 40, 41
Jahiz (Al), the philologist, 47, 58, 59
Jami's 'Beharistan,' 188
Jarir, the poet, 77, 78, 80
Jawini's 'Negaristan,' 188
Jeihani, the geographer, 49, 51
Jerusalem, the early Kiblah, 133 : changed to Mecca, 136
Jesus compared with Buddha, 142 : no details about his early career, 143
Jones (Sir William), 29
Jurisconsults, The seven, 36 (Obaid Allah, Orwa, Kasim, Said, Sulaiman, Abu Bakr, Kharija.)

K.

Kaabah, The, at Mecca, 3, 122, 144
Kab-bin-Zoheir, the poet, 31-33
Kali (Al), the philologist and author, 87, 103
Kama (Al), the poet, 30, 77
'Kama Sutra' of Vatsyayana, 182
Karitha, the hostile poetess, 31
Kasidas, i.e., Arab idyls or elegies, 28, 29
Kasim bin Asbagh, the traditionist, 38

Kasim (Al) bin Ma'an, the philologist and author, 59
'Katha Sarit Sagara,' The, 153, 154, 181-184 ; translated by Professor Tawney, 181 ; compared with the 'Arabian Nights,' 181 ; divided into 124 chapters, containing 330 stories, 182 ; their nature, 181-183
Khafaji, the poet, 117
Khaief al Ahmer, the author, 58
Khalid bin Barmek, 99
Khalid bin Walid, the general, 4, 129, 137, 147
Khalid bin Yazid, the alchemist, 40
Khalil (Al), the grammarian, 46, 47
'Khalilah wa Dimnah,' a story-book, 151-153
Kiblah, The, changed to Mecca, 136
Kindi (Al), or Alchendius, the philosopher, 24, 25, 65, 66
Kisai (Al), the grammarian, 47, 225
Koraish, tribe of, 2, 124, 125, 128, 134
Koran, The, 3, 23, 24, 138 : quotation from the 26th chapter, 31 ; as defined by the Muslims, 138 ; its division into chapters, 138 ; how it represents Muhammad, 138 ; not arranged until after his death, 138 ; as compared with our Bible, 132 : as described by Mr. Badger, 140, 141 ; as a literary composition, 142
Kosta bin Luka, the philosopher and physician, 65, 75, 91
Kuenen (Dr. A.), on the religion of Israel, 146, note
Kutrub, the grammarian and philologist, 60

L.

Labid, the poet, 29 ; his conversion, 34
Lane, a translator of the 'Nights,' 155
Lokman, the sage, 26, 27

M.

Madaini (Al), the historian, 53

16—2

Mahdi (Al), the Khalif, 19, 96, 98, 99
Majridi (Al), the philosopher, 65, 106
'Makamat Hariri,' 87, 88
Makin (Al), the chronicler, 97
Makkari (Al), the historian, 10, 22, 96, 117
Makrisi (Al), the historian and geographer, 110
Malik, the imam, 37
Mamun (Al), the Khalif, 12, 19, 74, 90, 96, 101
Mansur (Al), the Khalif, 12, 19, 73, 90, 96, 98, 99
Marwan II., the Khalif, 7, 19
Maseweih, the physician and translator, 75, 91
Masudi (Al), the historian, 53, 54
Mervezi (Al), the geographer, 49
'Merzuban-namah,' The, 192; extracts from it, 193-201
Mir Ali, the penman, 113
Moawia I., the Khalif, 5, 19, 33
Mofaddhal (Al), the compiler and editor of poems, 76, 85, 86
Montague (E. Wortley), his 'Nights,' 177, 178
Moors, The, in Spain, 9; their expulsion, 11, 112
Morell, a translator, 154
Moses compared with Muhammad, 142; as a liberator and organizer, 113, 145; why he stayed in the desert, 115; his legislation there, 116; to him the Jews owe their nationality, 146
Mothanna, the general, 4, 147
'Mua'llakat,' The, or suspended poems, 24, 28, 30
Mubarrad (Al), the grammarian, 18
Muhammad, the Apostle, 3, 18; his birth, 120; details of his life, 120-132; his death, 132; as a poet, 24, 30; as a reformer, preacher and apostle at Mecca, 119, 120, 132; as a military leader, 147; his military expeditions, 127-131, 147; his failure at Mecca, 131; his success at Madinah, 135, 136; his power there as Pope-King, 135; his virtues at Mecca, his vices at Madinah, 136; his wives, 122, 125, 127, 128, 129, 137; his concubines, 128, 129, 137; reasons for his numerous marriages, 137; compared with Moses, 142; to him the Arabs owe their nationality, 146; always insisted on faith and prayer, 149; his parting address at Mina, 150; his immediate successors, 4, 5, 18, 25; his companions and their successors, 39; his converts, 123, 124, 126, 129
Muhammad Al-Amin, the philologist and lawyer, 116
Muhammad bin Habib, the editor of poems, 76
Muhammad bin Saad, the historian, 53
Muhammad Hussain Tabrizi, the penman, 113
Muir (Sir William), 120; his life of Muhammad, 120, 137; his annals of the early Khalifate, 147
Munkah, the Sanscrit translator, 91
Musa, the general, 7
Musa bin Khalid, the translator, 91
Muslim Homeir, the geographer, 49
Musset (Alfred de), the poet, 233; the verses on his tomb in Paris, 234
Mustaa'sim (Al) Billah, the Khalif, 12, 20, 107
Mustatraf (Al), a story-book, 201; extracts from it, 202-209
Muta, Battle at, 130
Mutanabbi (Al), the poet, 77, 84, 85
Mysticism, 95

N.

Nabiga, the poet, 30
Nadim (An), author of the 'Fihrist,' 55, 56, 84, 85
Nami (An), the poet, 77, 85
'Naphat-ul-Yaman,' a story-book, 188; extracts from it, 188-192
Nasir-uddin-Tusy, the Persian, 107
Natural history, writers about, 58 (Khalef-al-Ahmer, Ahmad bin ud Dinveri, Jahiz (Al), Ibn Duraid, Shaibani (As), each indexed separately.)
Newton and the Bible, 110
Nulakht, the translator, 98

INDEX.

O.

Obaid Allah bin Jahsh, the Hanyf, 133
Ohud, Battle of, 127
Omaiyide Khalifs, Abd-ul-Malik and Walid I., patrons of literature and art, 95
Omaiyides, The, list of, 19 ; dynasty established, 5 ; conquests of, 6 ; fall of, 7
Omar, the Khalifah, 4, 19, 137, 147
Oriental Congress of 1889, v., vi.
Oriental lectures established, vi.
Oriental literature, study of, vi.
Oriental Translation Fund, Old, vi., vii. ; its revival, vi. ; new fund to be permanent, vii. ; some of its works, 54, 57, 88, 109, 115, 117 ; list of works published by, Appendix, 235
Otbi (Al), the poet, 77, 80, 82
Othman, the Khalifah, 4, 19
Othman bin Huwairith, the Hanyf, 133
Othman bin Talha, the custodian of the Kaabah, 3, 129
Oweis Al Keremi, the mystic, 95

P.

'Pancha Tantra,' 151, 153, 183
Passion Play, the Arab, 6
Payne (John), description of his 'Nights,' 155, 156, 175, 177, 180
Pelly (Sir Lewis), a translator, 6
Periods of Arab literature—first, 25 ; second, 30 ; third, 106 ; of Arab history, 2
Persia, its severance from the Abbasides, 13
Persian Portraits, 151
Petis de la Croix, a translator, 154
Philologists, Arab, 59
 (Kasim bin Ma'an, Kutrub, Jahiz (Al), Shaibani (As), Asmai (Al), Abu Obaida, Ansari (Al), Abu Othman, Abul Aina, Ibn Kutaiba, Ibn Duraid, each indexed separately.)
Philology, Arab, 59
Philosophers, Arab, 65
 (Khalid bin Yazid, Kindi (Al), Farabi (Al), Ibn Sina, Ali bin Ridhwan, Ghazali (Al), Ibn Bajah, Ibn Rashid, Kosta bin Luka, Thaleb bin Korra, Tavhidi (Al), Majridi (Al), each indexed separately.)
Philosophy, Arab, 64
Physicians, Arab, 72
 (Georgios bin Bakhtyeshun, Gabriel bin Georgios, Isa bin Musa, Maseweih, Yahya bin Maseweih, Honein bin Ishak, Kosta bin Luka, Razi, Ibn Batlan, each indexed separately.)
Places of learning, 105
Pococke, a translator, 97
Poem of the Mantle, by Kab bin Zoheir, 31, 33
Poem of the Mantle, by Al Busiri, 32, note
Poetry before Muhammad's time, 25, 28
Poetry, Collectors and editors of Arab, 76
 (Mofaddhal (Al), Shaibani (As), Abu Zaid bin A'us, Ibn as Sikkit, Muhammad bin Habib, Abu Hatim as Sejastani, Abu Othman al Mazini, Abu Tammam, Bohtori (Al), Ibn-ul-Marzaban, Ibn Demash, Zukkari, Abu Bakr as-Sauli, Abul Faraj al-Ispahani, each indexed separately.)
Poets, Arab, 28, 30, 77
 (Amriolkais, Antara, Labid, Tarafa, Amru, Harath, Zoheir, Nabiga, Kama (Al), Aasha (Al), Akhtal (Al), Farazdak, Jarir, Abul-Atahya, Bashshar bin Burd, Abu Nuwas, Abu Tammam, Otbi (Al), Bohtori (Al), Mutanabbi (Al), Nami (An), each indexed separately.)
Printing presses of Arabic to-day, 118
Prophets mentioned by Muhammad, 133
Purgstall (Von Hammer), author and translator, 96, 155

Q.

Quaritch (Bernard), his catalogue, vii.

R.

Radhi (Al) Billah, the Khalif, 20, 101, 102
Razi, or Rhazes, the physician, 24, 25, 75
Redhouse (J. W.), the translator, 32
Rehatsek (E.), the translator, viii., 30, 53
Reiske, a translator, 97
Remarks, Introductory, v.
Rénan, extracts from, 144, 145
Rodiger, a translator, 27
Rückert, a translator, 89

S.

Sacey de (Baron Silvestre), 26, 89, 108
Sad bin Malik, the general, 4
Sa'di's 'Gulistan,' 188
Sayuti (Jalal-uddin), the Egyptian author, 111
Scott (Jonathan), a translator, 155, 177, 178
Sehl bin Nubakht, 90
Seville, 9
Shafai (Al), the imam, 37
Shaibani (Abu Amr as), the grammarian, philologist, writer on natural history, and editor of poems, 49, 60, 76
Shiahs, Description of the, 5
Sibawaih, the grammarian, 46, 47
'Sihr-ul-oyoon,' a book on the eye, 210; extracts from it, 210-212
'Siraj-ul Muluk,' an interesting work, 212; extracts from it, 212-216
Society of the Brethren of Purity, 105
Sofyan at Thauri, an imam, 38
Somadeva (Bhatta), an Indian author, 182, 183
Soudanese, The, 148
Spain, Omaiyide rulers in, 21; other rulers, 8: the Almoravides, 9; the Almohades, 9
Spanish Omaiyide Khalifs, 8, 21; the two greatest, Abd-ar-Rahman III. and Hakim II., 102
Sprenger (Dr. A.), a translator, 54
Stories from Ibn Khallikan, 217-228

Stories from the 'Arabian Nights,' 157-174
Stories from the 'Merzuban-namah,' 193-201
Stories from the 'Mustatraf,' 202-209
Stories from the 'Naphut-ul-Yaman,' 188-192
Stories from the 'Sihr-ul-oyoon,' 210-212
Stories from the 'Siraj-ul-Muluk,' 212-216
Stories from various sources, 228-233
Sulaiman, the lawgiver, 112, 116
Sunnis, Description of the, 5
Syria and Palestine, 14; conquest of, by the Fatimites, 14; by the Seljuks, 14; by Saladin, 15; by Selim I., 15

T.

Tabari, the historian, 53
Taki-uddin of Fez, the historian, 110
Tarafa, the poet, 29
Tarik, the general, 7
Tavhidi (Al), the philosopher, 65, 106
Tawney (C. H.), the translator, 181
Testaments, our Old and New, 133, 139
Thalab, the grammarian, 48
Thalab bin Korra, the philosopher, 65
Theophilus of Edessa, the translator, 98
'Thousand and one Nights,' 152, 154-156, 174-176
Torrens, a translator of the 'Nights,' 155
Tradition, The six Fathers of, 38 (Al-Bukhari, Muslim, At-Tirmidi, Abu Dawud, An-Nasai, Ibn Majah.)
Traditionists, Early, 38
Traditionists, Minor, 38
Translations, how carried on, 90, 91, 98
Translators, 89-91 (Ibn-Al Mukaffa, Abd-allah bin Hilal, Sehl bin Nubakht, Musa bin Khalid, Yusuf bin Khalid, Hassan bin Sehl, Baladori

INDEX. 247

(Al), Munkah, the Indian, Ibn Washiyah, Honein bin Ishak, Maseweih and his son Yahya, Kosta bin Luka, Theophilus of Edessa, each indexed separately.)
Travellers, see 'Geographers'
Trebutien, a translator, 155

U.

Ulema, Establishment of the, 116

V.

Vatsyayana, the Hindoo author of the 'Kama Sutra,' 182
Voltaire and the Bible, 140
'Vrihat Katha,' or Great Tale, 182, 183

W.

Wackidi (Al), the historian, 53
Walid I., the sixth Omaiyide Khalif, 7, 19
Warakah, the Hanyf, 123, 132
Weil (Dr.), the translator, 53, 155
White (Dr Joseph), 177

World, End of the, prophesied, 111
Wüstenfeld (Dr.), the editor and author, 52, 76

Y.

Yahya bin Khalid, the Barmekide, 99, 100
Yahya bin Maseweih, the physician and translator, 74, 75, 91, 98
Yakut, the penman, 113, 114
Yazid I., the second Omaiyide Khalif, 5, 6, 19
Yusuf bin Khalid, the translator, 91

Z.

Zaid, the inquirer, 132
Zihary, the hostile poet, 31
Ziuzerling, a translator, 155
Zobeida, the wife of Harun-ar-Rashid, 97, 108
Zoheir, the poet, 29
Zotenberg (H.), of the Bibliothèque Nationale, Paris, 176, 177, 179
Zukkari, the editor of poems, 76

THE END.

BILLING AND SONS, PRINTERS, GUILDFORD.

MR. WILLIAM HEINEMANN'S LIST.

THE BONDMAN: A New Saga. By HALL CAINE, Author of 'The Deemster.' Three volumes, crown 8vo., 31s. 6d. Third Edition. At all Libraries.

'It is impossible to deny originality and rude power to this saga, impossible not to admire its forceful directness and the colossal grandeur of its leading characters.'—*Times*.
'It is a splendid novel.'—*Academy*.
'Three volumes of crowded incidents.'—*Athenæum*.
'Reaches a level to which fiction very rarely attains.'—*Speaker*.
'Distinctly ahead of all fictional literature of our time.'—*Scotsman*.
'Sublime in its poetry, intense in its pathos, instinct with resistless passion.'—*Liverpool Mercury*.

HAUNTINGS: Fantastic Stories. By VERNON LEE, Author of 'Baldwin,' 'Miss Brown,' etc. One volume, crown 8vo., 6s.

CONTENTS: Amour Dure—Dionea : in the Country of Venus—Oke of Okehurst : A Phantom Lover—A Wicked Voice.

A VERY STRANGE FAMILY: A Novel. By F. W. ROBINSON, Author of 'Grandmother's Money,' 'Lazarus in London,' etc. One volume, crown 8vo., 3s. 6d.

IDLE MUSINGS : Essays in Social Mosaic. By E. CONDER GRAY, Author of 'Wise Words and Loving Deeds,' etc. One Volume, crown 8vo., 6s.

'Light, brief, and bright are the "essays in social Mosaic." Mr. Gray ranges like a butterfly from high themes to trivial with a good deal of dexterity, and a profusion of illustration.'—*Saturday Review*.
'Pleasantly written, will serve admirably to while away an idle half-hour or two.'—*Graphic*.
'Never dull or wearisome, but full of genuine humour.'—*Newcastle Chronicle*.
'Hits the nail on the head.'—*Speaker*.

THE GARDEN'S STORY ; or, Pleasures and Trials of an Amateur Gardener. By G. H. ELLWANGER. With an Introduction by the Rev. C. WOLLEY DOD. One volume, fcap. 8vo., Illustrated, 5s.

MR. WILLIAM HEINEMANN'S LIST—continued.

ARABIC AUTHORS: A Manual of Arabian History and Literature. By F. F. ARBUTHNOT, M.R.A.S., Author of 'Early Ideas' and 'Persian Portraits.' One volume, post 8vo., 10s.

IVY AND PASSION FLOWER: Poems. By GERARD BENDALL, Author of 'Estelle,' etc. One volume, fcap. 8vo, 3s. 6d.

INDIA, AND OUR RESPONSIBILITIES AND DUTIES AS CITIZENS OF THE EMPIRE. A Political Tract for the Times. By CYRIL S. COBB, B.C.L., M.A. Post 8vo., wrapper, 1s.

STUDIES OF RELIGIOUS HISTORY. By ERNEST RENAN. Authorised Translation, from the latest Revised and Corrected Edition. One volume, post 8vo., 10s. 6d.

IN THE PRESS.

THE MOMENT AFTER. By ROBERT BUCHANAN. Fcap. 8vo., wrapper, 1s.

THE MASTER OF THE MAGICIANS: A Novel. By ELIZABETH STUART PHELPS and HERBERT D. WARD. One volume, imperial 16mo.

COME FORTH! A Story of the Time of Christ. By ELIZABETH STUART PHELPS and HERBERT D. WARD. One volume, imperial 16mo.

PASSION THE PLAYTHING: A Novel. By R. MURRAY GILCHRIST. One volume, crown 8vo.

SKETCHES: Descriptive, Social, and Literary. By W. H. DAVENPORT ADAMS. Reprinted by permission from the *Illustrated London News*. One volume, crown 8vo.

THE GENESIS OF THE UNITED STATES. A Narrative of the Movement in England (1605-1616) which resulted in the Plantation of North America by Englishmen. A Collection of Historical Manuscripts, Rare Tracts, etc., with Notes, Plans, Maps, Portraits, Autographs, and a Bibliographical Index. Arranged and Edited by ALEXANDER BROWN, Fellow of the Royal Historical Society, Member of the Virginia Historical Society, and of the American Historical Association. Two volumes, 8vo.

21, BEDFORD STREET, LONDON, W.C.

www.ingramcontent.com/pod-product-compliance
Lightning Source LLC
Chambersburg PA
CBHW032147230426
43672CB00011B/2475